REMINISCENCES
OF THE
TWENTIETH CENTURY

VOLUME I

2/13/16

Peter P. Genero

Other Books by Peter P. Genero

THANK ROSENDALE (New York - The Empire State)

HANDBOOK FOR LECTORS

REMINISCENCES OF THE TWENTIETH CENTURY
VOLUME I

Publisher: GENERO Inc.
               1904 York Court
               Fort Pierce, FL 34982
               Email: ppgenero@aol.com

Printed in the United Sates of America

ISBN: 0-9759419-2-5

Cover: PFC Peter P. Genero; Los Angeles, CA , Circa 1942

REMINISCENCES OF THE TWENTIETH CENTURY
VOLUME I

CONTENTS

CHAPTER

REMINISCENCES OF THE TWENTIETH CENTURY - VOLUME II

CONTENTS (TENATIVE)

ILLUSTRATIONS

COVER: Peter P. Genero, Author; Circa 1942

PROLOGUE

This book is not intended to be an autobiography. Its purpose is to highlight certain events in which the author was involved, either directly or indirectly, and which the reader may find interesting. Some of the specifics may be questioned, but they are exactly as remembered by the author to the best of his knowledge and belief. Where appropriate they were confirmed by other sources.

CHAPTER 1

PETER P. GENERO

The author was born on April 4, 1921, in the house shown in the attached photograph. It had been the lock tender's house for lock # 7 of the old Delaware and Hudson (D & H) Canal.

The principal features of the photograph are:

1. The large yellow/white main house (13 rooms).

2. The small white house attached to the right side of the main house is the well house. In it, the water flowed continually, 24 hours a day, 7 days a week, 365 days a year. The water came from a nearby deep well. It was cool, clear, fresh drinking water, which never stopped flowing.

3. Attached to the house on the left is a large white enclosed porch. It was used for recreational purposes. In the summer, it served also as an outdoor dining room.

4. The large red barn had been built as a shelter and feed stop for the mules and horses, which pulled the canal barges.

5. On the extreme left is the family chicken coop.

6. In the foreground is the Rondout Creek, which played such an important role in the lives of the Genero Family.

Genero Homestead
Certificate of Birth, Peter Genero
Certificate of Baptism, Peter Genero
Genero Family Tree, 1888-1999

Courtesy: Genero Family Collection   GENERO HOMESTEAD ROSENDALE, NY; Circa 1960

Form VS-10. (REV. 2/68)

CERTIFICATION OF BIRTH
DEPARTMENT OF HEALTH
STATE OF NEW YORK

District No. 5523

Registered No. 6

THIS IS TO CERTIFY that PeTeR GeNeRo Ju.

sex Male was born on APRIL 4 on 19 21

in Rosendale N-y , County of U lster

and State of New York, as shown by the record of birth filed 4 - 9 , 19 21

with the registrar of vital statistics of this registration district.

Witness my signature this 19 day of Sept 19 72

Catherine O'Leary

Registrar of Vital Statistics

City
Village of Rosendale , New York
Town

WARNING: Any Alteration Invalidates This Certificate

3

Certificate of Baptism

✝

Church of

St. Peter

Saundale, N.Y.

This is to certify

That _Peter Genero_

Child of _Peter Genero_

and _Mary Stychovich_

born on the _7_ day of _April_ _1921_

was **Baptized**

on the _17th_ day of _April_ _1921_

According to the Rite of the Roman Catholic Church

by the Rev. _John J. Sehfton C.SS.R_

the Sponsors being { _Charles Nalli_
Margaret McCreavy

as appears from the Baptismal Register of this Church.

Dated _Sept. 1, 1937_

_____ Pastor.

NO. 814. F. J. BERNET CO. NEW YORK

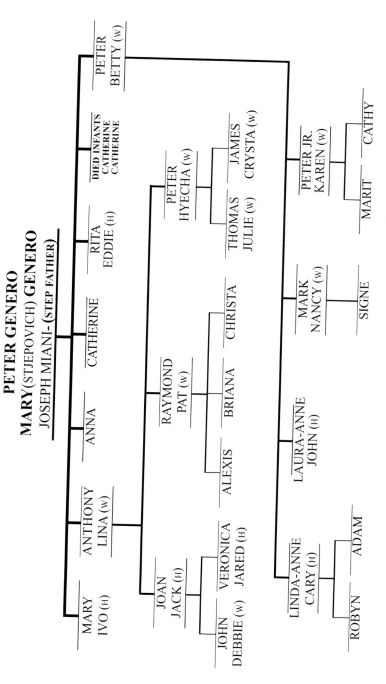

PETER GENERO
MARY(STJEPOVICH) **GENERO**
JOSEPH MIANI- **(STEP FATHER)**

GENERO FAMILY TREE - 20th Century

5

CHAPTER 2

EARLY YEARS IN ROSENDALE

Preface:

The saddest event to take place during this period was the passing away of my father in 1922. This left my mother a widow with six children, ages 1 thru 17.

In 1925, she married a hard-rock miner called "Joe" (a name he insisted on being called). Joe was a big, powerful miner who, at that time, was working in Rosendale in a tunnel through the Shawangunk mountains. Its purpose was to bring water from the large Ashokan Reservoir in the Catskill Mountains, to the city of New York

Economic conditions of the family improved significantly.

Early Years
Rosendale Union Free School

Early Years:

Photograph - Genero Family Collection
PETER GENERO-ROSENDALE, NY; Circa 1926

The photo shows the author standing in the snow, on the tow path of the Delaware and Hudson Canal, in front of his home (not shown). The house in the background was really an old barn in which grain was stored to feed the horses and mules that pulled the canal boats. Later our neighbors converted the barn into their home. In the far background, is the old Walkill Valley Railroad Bridge. When built, it was considered to be one of the highest bridges in the state of New York (approx 130 feet). Faintly visible behind the bridge is the Joppenburg Mountain, site of the famous "Miracle of Rosendale." The mountain had been undermined to such an extent that it imploded, closing all shafts and tunnels. The "miracle": no casualities.

Since I do not remember having a new pair of boots, the ones I was wearing probably belonged to my sister.

The first interesting experience that I had during this period was, when at the age of four, I disappeared from the Kingston City Hospital.

In order to support the family at that time, my mother took a job as a cook in the Kingston City Hospital, 8 miles from Rosendale. Since I was too young to attend school, my mother took me with her by train to the hospital each day. While my mother worked, I was placed in a suitable corner of the kitchen and given some blocks, boxes, etc., with which to amuse myself.

When my mother had to leave the kitchen for a period of time, I was immobilized with a suitable restraint. Normally, it was with a length of thin rope. One end was fastened to me, and the other end to a leg of the kitchen sink.

One day my mother returned to the kitchen and found her son missing. Somehow I had managed to disengage myself from my fetters. Immediately, a search was instituted by my mother, members of the hospital staff, and even some of the nurses. After a period of anxiety, my whereabouts was discovered.

I had left the hospital and had gone to a neighbor's house, which had a rocking chair on its porch. A member of the hospital staff found me there. I can still recall that happy and pleasant feeling I experienced while I was rocking myself back and forth in that rocking chair.

Years later, I wondered if this incident was not the origin of my wanderlust and love of travel.

Rosendale Union Free School:

My other interesting memories of these early years concerned my attendance at the Rosendale Union Free School. The Rosendale school was the "lead school" in the township. It had two classrooms: one for grades 1-4 and the other for grades 5-8. The other six schools in the township had only one classroom.

This was the era before school buses, and all students had to walk to school. To alleviate the problem, the schools were located in a checker board fashion throughout the township. As a result, no student had to walk more than two miles to school. For me, this was fortunate since my walking distance was slightly less than one mile. In the Rosendale school house class room, there were four rows of desks. The first row was for the first grade; the second row was for the second grade, etc.. One interesting feature concerning the desks was that they were "double desks." They were wide enough so that two students could sit side by side. In other words, a row of six desks could accommodate up to 12 students. The first grade did not use pen, paper, or ink. Their lessons were written with chalk on small individual slate blackboards.

The most enjoyable times were during recess, one in the morning and one in the afternoon. The usual games were played, and they were especially fun during snow times. Of course, the pupils who mis-behaved during class had to stay indoors, clean the blackboards, and "clap" the erasers until they were dust free. The sole source of heating during the winter was a round pot-bellied stove in the rear of the classroom.

The manner in which a teacher handled multiple classes in a single room was quite simple, but very tedious for the teacher. The teacher would explain a lesson (reading, writing, and arithmetic), to the first row, and then give them a lengthy practice assignment. Then she would do the same for the second row, then the third row, etc.. Of the four grades, one was always being taught a new lesson, while the other three grades were practicing their given assignments.

An incident took place that year, which will give the reader a better understanding of the flexible manner in which a small country school operated. There were only two students in the fourth grade, my sister Rita (the bright one of the family), and a local boy, who was not known for his academic achievements. Not desiring to teach only two students in a single grade, my sister was advanced to the fifth grade, and the other student was sent back to the third grade. That year there was no fourth grade in the Rosendale school.

In addition to school, life in general continued along typical country lines.

In the spring, we picked berries and helped plant the garden. In the fall, we gathered hickory nuts and played in large piles of brightly colored autumn leaves. These were in addition to our usual duties of chopping wood, hauling water, etc.

In winter, darkness arrived early, around 4 PM, and temperatures of ten degrees below zero were not uncommon. Indoors, we occupied ourselves with playing dominos, checkers, and board games, such parcheesi and tiddlywinks. Our innovative mother helped with organizing popcorn roasts, taffy pulling evenings, and sometimes helping us make pans of fudge.

Outdoor winter nights were often fun and enjoyable. Big Joe built us a large, steerable bob-sled. On bright moon light nights, we went sleigh riding. We pulled the bob sled up to the top of Binnewater Hill, and almost the entire family climbed aboard. Then we rode the sleigh down the hill, singing and shouting. Sometimes, even Big Joe did the steering. We went down hill so fast that at the bottom we coasted quite some distance out onto the main highway. At that time, vehicular travel at night and in the winter was rare.

All of this changed when we moved to the city.

CHAPTER 3

PRE -TEEN YEARS IN NEW YORK CITY

Preface:

In 1927, the family (mother, stepfather, one brother and four sisters) moved to New York City. The family home in Rosendale was retained under the care of our old "nanny" Katie Madden.

Big Joe got a job as a foreman of a tunneling crew building the new 8th Avenue subway in New York City. With the two older sisters working on Wall Street, the family was living quite well.

It was at this time that the family had the house in Rosendale wired for electricity (no more kerosene lamps). The family also bought its first automobile, a 1928 Chevrolet, four door sedan, with green solid rim wheels. We also bought our first radio, a large battery powered set with an enormous loud speaker. It was over this set that we heard the wonderful news of Lindbergh's safe landing in Paris.

This comfortable living lasted until about 1933, when construction of the 8th Avenue subway was completed and the country was in the midst of a Great Depression. It was then that the family made a difficult decision. It was decided that Mother and Big Joe would return to Rosendale and convert the family house into a boarding house. The other members of the family would remain in the city and continue their schooling and/or working on Wall Street.

There was much traveling back and forth, especially during the holidays. All of those who were attending school spent their summers in Rosendale helping with the boarding house.

We were a closely knit family, with an ingrained deep affection for one another. The following incident will illustrate these characteristics.

During our early days in the city, I became ill and had to remain home for several weeks. Catherine, one of my older sisters, was attending Cathedral High School, about 20 - 30 city blocks from our apartment. She was given ten cents each day so that she could take the 6th Avenue "EL" to and from school. However, every day during my illness, rain or shine, she would walk to and from school and save the ten cents. On her way home, she would stop at Woolworth's 5 and 10 cents store and buy a small toy. When she got home, she would give me the toy to help take my mind off my illness.

Life in the City
Saint Paul's Church and School
Games Kids Played in the City
Summers in Rosendale (Part I)
The Great Depression

Life in the City:

Initially, the family lived in a six room apartment on Amsterdam (10th) Avenue near 63d Street. This area of the city was chosen because there were a number of my parent's "old country" friends living in that area.

The apartment was one flight up in an old tenement type building. It was reasonably comfortable for that era. In the kitchen was a large copper hot water tank, which required hours of hard scrubbing to keep it shiny, Also in the kitchen, were a wood/coal stove, sink, and an old fashioned "ice box." A large chunk of ice, purchased biweekly, kept the food reasonably cool in the summer. In the winter an exterior metal "window box" was used. The apartment was equipped with an exterior pulley type clothes line. It was in an airshaft that was accessible from one of our apartment windows. Residents of other apartments had to carry their wet clothes up to roof and hang them on clothes lines attached to couple of iron pipes.

Within a few blocks were a multitude of public transportation systems. These included the 6th and 9th Avenue elevated trains; the 10th Avenue electric trolley cars; the IRT, BMT, and Independent subway systems; and a multitude of bus lines, including the famed 5th Avenue double-decker buses. For only a nickel, one could travel to almost any part of the metropolitan area. There was no need for an automobile in the city, and very few people owned one.

As usual, our mother was the heart and soul of the family, working from morning into the night. In addition, she worked as a cook for one the legendary Schrafts restaurants, which were very popular at that time. What tasks she could not do, she assigned to one of the members of the family.

I was the "go-for" and errand runner for the family. I did the shopping at nearby family-owned stores and produce push carts which lined the streets. On Saturdays, I had to help clean the house. It was interesting in that my brother and I wished to finish early so that we could go out and play. Since my sisters had more tasks to perform and since it took them much longer to complete, we had to devise a mutually agreeable working plan. We divided the kitchen/dining room in half. My brother and I would finish our half and go out to play. Our sisters would not finish their half till late in the afternoon. Saturday visitors were surprised to see only one half of the kitchen/dining room floor scrubbed clean.

Another task, which I was assigned, was that of gathering kindling wood for the stove. As early as possible each Saturday, I made a tour of all of the stores and vegetable markets in the area, looking for discarded wooden boxes and crates. These I took down into the cellar and chopped into kindling. Sometimes, I would even go all the way to the railroad freight yards on 12th Avenue to look for pieces of wood discarded from box cars.

A major change took place in 1934 as the result of a fire in the Pawn Shop below. Not much was lost in our apartment, but all of our clothes and belongings suffered water and smoke damage. Saddest of all was the loss of Jamey, the prettiest and best singing canary that we ever owned.

The family moved to an apartment that was in a little more up-scale neighborhood. It is now the site of The Lincoln Cultural Center. The apartment had steam heat in all of the rooms, and a bathroom within. (We no longer had to use the one in the hallway). The kitchen had an electric refrigerator and gas stove. There was even a carpet on the stairs in the entrance.

Later, when I finished high school and there were only four of us living in the city. We moved to, what was at that time, a really nice neighborhood in Woodside, Long Island. There were even trees planted along the sidewalks.

Saint Paul's Church and School:

Saint Paul's Church and Grade School were adjacent to each other and part of the same complex. They were located between 59th and 60th Streets in Manhattan, about one block from Columbus Circle. Also, they were between Columbus (9th) Avenue and Amsterdam (10th) Avenue. My formative years revolved around these two centers of activity.

It appears that I was a slow learner. When our family moved to New York City, I attended Saint Paul's grade school. Upon arrival and after some consultation, it was decided that I should repeat the first grade all over again. The excuse given was that I was only six years old and that I should be with my contemporaries. In Rosendale, one started school at five years of age, but in New York City, a child did not start school until six years of age.

I attended services in the church and served as an altar boy. Later I became closely involved with social and church related activities, which continued until I left for military service in 1941. It was in this environment that lasting relationships were formed, which have remained till the present day.

Saint Paul's Church was second in size only to Saint Patrick's Cathedral. It was the home of the Paulist Fathers, missionaries for the rapidly expanding number of Catholics in the United States. They also sent missionaries to foreign countries. Perhaps it was most renown for its world famed choir. Besides giving numerous concerts in Carnegie Hall, the choir performed in many foreign countries. It was featured on the sound track of one of the most famous movies of that time, *The Tale Of Two Cities*.

Saint Paul's School on 60th street, was quite large, 1,000+ students, boys and girls in separate classes. It was run by the Sisters of the Holy Cross, a traditional order of nuns. They wore full length black habits, with large white celluloid collars and head pieces. Classes were taught in the no nonsense manner of the famed Catholic schools of the last century. They were assisted by several lay teachers of equal ability. All were totally dedicated to their profession, and their results were truly outstanding. Proof of their effectiveness can be shown by comparing the scores of their students on the state regents examinations, with those of the public school students.

The Catholic school scores were significantly higher, despite the fact that their school year was 3 to 4 weeks shorter. For Saint Paul's school, this was a singular accomplishment, since most of the students came from the "less affluent" areas of the city.

As could be expected, the two smartest students in our class went on to become priests. Jimmy Lloyd became a Paulist Father, and Paul Callahan became a Jesuit.

School hours were from 9 AM till 3 PM. One hour was allowed at noon, so the students could go home for lunch. If it was raining at noon, classes continued till 1 PM. The students were then dismissed for the day. Naturally, the students looked forward to rainy days.

Students were not permitted to roam about freely in the school building. Prior to class, they were assembled in front of the school on 60th Street. When the first bell rang, they lined up in the street by class. When the second bell rang, they were marched to their respective classrooms. For dismissal, the order was reversed. The students were marched out onto the street and then dismissed. Within the school building, a sense of quiet and orderly discipline was maintained.

As can be seen from the graduation class picture, page 19, there were 43 male students in our class. Unlike modern schools, a large number of students in a class, was not considered an impediment to learning. Also at that time, students who could not "keep up" were simply not promoted.

I was a moderate in class studies. The high point came when I was selected to be trained as an altar boy. This was not a simple task. At that time, mass was celebrated in the Latin Rite. The altar boy was required to memorize all of the lengthy responses in Latin. It was also a matter of dedication, since early masses began at 5 AM (rain or snow not withstanding). In one sense, being an altar boy was similar to school. One started out serving individual "low" masses. Then, he was advanced to serving at "high" masses and other religious services. One started out by being a Torch Bearer. Then he was promoted to Acolyte, Cross Bearer, Thurifer, etc,. The results of this training have remained with me till the present day.

As can be imagined, the eight years at Saint Paul's School were quite routine: school, homework, play, housework, etc., each day. Probably the two most enjoyable events of this period were my two visits to the Old Madison Square Garden. On one visit, I saw a performance of the famous Barnum & Bailey Three Ring Circus. On the other visit, I watched part of a Six Day Bike Race.

It might also be mentioned that during this period there were two other incidents, which may be worthy of note:

1) In June 1934, New York City welcomed the arrival of the United States Navy. All ships were open to visits by the public. The celebration was inaugurated with a massive flight of naval aircraft over the city. It may sound strange today, but most of the aircraft were "biplanes" some of which had open cockpits. I spent many, many hours waiting in line for a chance to board the ships and walk through them. The easiest ships to board were the aircraft carriers, Lexington and Saratoga. They were tied up to the Hudson River pier on 53d Street. The lines were not too long and one simply had to walk up the gang plank to the boarding deck.

The battleships were a different matter. They were anchored out in the middle of the Hudson River. Visitors had to wait on shore for long periods before being able to climb into a small skiff, which took them out to the battleships. I remembered three things from these visits: all ships were spotlessly clean; some of the battleships still had wooden decks; and sailors still slept in canvas hammocks suspended from overhead beams.

Later, two of the battleships, the USS Pennsylvania and the USS West Virginia, achieved immortality. They were sunk or damaged at Pearl Harbor.

2) The class outing for the graduating class (see class photo next page) was a bus ride to Coney Island. There, the owner of Steeplechase Park gave each student a complimentary 50 ride ticket. It included the roller coaster, Ferris wheel, mechanical horse racing, electric bumper car rides, etc. A wonderfully exciting time was had by all. However, there were two exceptions. These two students came from the less affluent neighborhood of our parish. It seems that they had no desire to ride in a crowded school bus. They "misappropriated" an automobile and tried to follow the school buses to Coney Island. They were picked up by the police in Brooklyn. Instead of graduating with their class, they were sent to the Catholic Protectory, a reform school under the auspices of the Archdiocese of New York.

Games Kids Played in the City:

We were fortunate in that we were only two blocks from Central Park. It was great for baseball, football, tree climbing, rock climbing, or what ever else we could conjure up. The enormous baseball field was about ten acres of packed dirt. It had about a half dozen backstops and regular baseball diamonds, which were for the older players. Of most importance, there was the large space between the marked-off fields. In this space, any bunch of kids could play any type of baseball they desired. It was not unusual to see as many as 15 - 20 little groups playing at the same time. The space used was on a first come, first serve basis. Everyone seemed satisfied and no major disputes arose.

This all changed about 1935 when the Park Commissioner, Robert Moses, got into the act. It seemed that the enormous packed dirt field did not meet his esthetic requirements. He converted the big packed dirt field into about six manicured baseball diamonds,

Photograph - Genero Family Collection

Graduation Class - 1935 - Saint Paul's Catholic School
Author, First Row, Second to the right of Father Robert, School director

19

with pitcher's mounds, regular bases, mowed grass, and marked-off fowl lines. It certainly up-graded the baseball field.

HOWEVER, the field was reserved for officially recognized baseball leagues and teams. Without a park permit, no one was allowed to play on the field, and especially not between the diamonds. This left our team and the other "sand lot" teams with no place to play except on 11th Avenue and 53rd street. This was a two square block area of packed dirt in the middle of "Hells Kitchen."

As a result, Central Park was no longer our primary play area. This honor went to 60th Street, between Columbus (9th) Avenue and Amsterdam (10th) Avenue. This was not as bad as it might seem.

This portion of 60th Street was designated a "play street." There were barricades at both ends and no thru traffic was permitted. Saint Paul's School was also located there. It should be remembered that this was the era before mass automobile transportation. Few people in the city owned automobiles, especially in this neighborhood. Horse and wagons were widely used. Horse drawn wagons were still the primary vehicles used for delivering milk, ice and bakery products. At that time, street cleaners were equipped with stiff brooms, shovels and two barreled trash carts. They did a reasonably good job of keeping the cross walks free of animal droppings.

Some of the games we played on 60th street were kick-the-can; box ball; ringaleerio; touch football; and most important of all, stick-ball.

Kick-the-can: It was similar to hide and seek. Upon being "spied", there was a race to see who could get home first and kick-the-can. If the person who was "IT" did not win the race, he had to start from the beginning all over again.

Box Ball: It was similar to baseball except that the batter hit a rubber ball with his fist or open hand, Also, the playing field was in the street, square, and only about 40 feet on a side.

Ringaleerio: For this game, the group was split into two teams. One side was "IT" and the other was free to roam all over. An "IT" team member had to run after a free member and touch him. If touched, the free team member had to go to the home box (a designated area about 10 feet square). This continued until all free team members were in the box. However, if a free team member could race to the box without being touched, then all members in the box were free, and the game would start all over again.

Touch Football: The same general rules applied as in normal touch football. The one exception (since no one owned a real football) was that a tightly wound roll of newspapers was used to simulate a football.

It was during this period that I was introduced to the YMCA. Each Saturday morning, the up-scale YMCA on Central Park West would open its doors to groups of less affluent kids from adjacent neighborhoods. At 10 AM , we would take a small bar of soap and towel, and show up at the "Y", as it was then called. There, we were permitted to play basketball on their beautiful, regulation size, indoor basketball court. Afterwards , we would take a shower in their very large shower room. Then, we would go swimming in their large, heated indoor swimming pool. We would emerge around noon, completely refreshed and clean. No need for our traditional "Saturday night" bath.

Marbles were also popular at that time. It was played in the street gutters, and "home" was on a round iron sewer cover.

Stick-ball: This was our most popular game, and it was unique to New York City. It was very similar to baseball. The diamond was long and narrow to conform to the street upon which it was being played. Iron sewer covers were located in the center of the street, about 300 feet apart. One sewer cover was home plate, and the next sewer cover was second base. First and third bases were usually stoop railings on opposite sides of the street. Generally, the rules were the same as baseball with a few modifications.

The ball used was a rubber "Spaulding." It was about the size of a tennis ball, but without the fuzz. The pitcher threw the ball to the batter on a bounce, with as much spin as he could manage. The bat was a long broom stick handle.

The batter waited for a pitch he liked, but he was given only one "swing." If a batted ball did not travel as far as the pitcher, in fair territory, the batter was out. The most aggravating problem was the exterior iron fire escapes attached to the tenement buildings. If a batted ball hit one, the bounce was unpredictable. Running bases was similar to baseball, except that base stealing was not allowed, and runners could not take a "lead" off base.

Every block had at least one stick ball team. Competition among the block teams was intense. The older guys played for sizeable stakes. A $100 game was not uncommon.

Stick ball received quite a notoriety in the city. I was surprised recently, while watching a documentary on television concerning New York City. It featured the Mayor's "Annual Stick-ball Game." What was really surprising was that the game was being played on 60th Street, using the same sewer covers as bases that we used, 70 years earlier.

As can be derived from the above, none of the kids of our age group from the neighborhood, went on to achieve fame in the sports world. Perhaps the one exception was Leo Romanello. He became a ranked middle-weight boxer and fought a number of fights in Madison Square Garden.

Summers in Rosendale (Part I):

During the 1930's and 1940's, our home in Rosendale became a boarding house. The house was fairly large and could accommodate about 10 - 12 boarders on a routine basis. On weekends, it was not unusual to have as many as 20-25 overnight boarders.

During the busy periods, the family slept in the barn, dormitory style: women downstairs and men upstairs. On occasion, the family and the Dubrovnik Club would sponsor a bus ride (30-40 participants) from the city to Rosendale.

This was the era before mega resorts with air-conditioned rooms, casinos, and accessible mass air transportation. In order to escape the high humidity and heat of the city, the city folks went to the Catskill Mountains, where the air was cooler, cleaner, and more comfortable. They traveled by automobile, bus, or train. There, they enjoyed a good night's rest, fine meals, comradeship, and hiking in the mountains. Fishing and swimming were very popular in the many lakes and streams in the area.

All of the above were available in Rosendale. However, the greatest claim to fame for our family boarding house was the superior and abundant food that was served. Also popular was the family's excellent home made wine that was served at all meals.

The forgoing was inserted to give the reader a glimpse into the boarding house era, which played such an important part in our lives in the 30's and 40's.

It was customary for the members of the family who were still attending school in the city, to travel to Rosendale on the first day of summer vacation. For me, this usually meant a solo bus ride to Rosendale, fare about 75 cents. This was before the massive Port Authority Bus Terminal had been built near the Lincoln Tunnel.

The most interesting part of the bus trip was watching the operation of the city terminal for the Rosendale buses. It was located in the basement of the old Dixie Hotel on 42d Street. The incoming buses entered the rear of the hotel on 43d Street. Then they went down a steep inclined ramp into the hotel basement. There, the bus stopped on a large circular iron roundtable.

The controller then rotated the roundtable until the bus was aligned with its proper stall, in order to load and unload its passengers. When leaving, the bus backed out onto the roundtable and was rotated until it was aligned with the steep exit ramp. I would just sit there and watch this marvel of modern machinery.

For the summers, our two oldest sisters stayed in the city and continued working at their stenographic jobs. My two other sisters, brother and I went to Rosendale as soon as our school vacations began. This resulted in a boarding house work force of our mother, step-father, two older sisters, one older brother, and myself.

The boarding house routine was as follows:

1) All boarders were assigned bed rooms. Otherwise, they had use of all common facilities and were free to roam inside and outside as they desired.

2) There were four meal times. Breakfast was served individually in the dining room , anytime before 9 AM. The noon and evening meals were served in the open porch. Mealtimes were announced by the ringing of the dinner bell. The mid afternoon coffee and cake were served under one of the grape arbors, on a casual self help basis.

3) Sleeping, resting, or other activities, were at the border's discretion.

It was during mealtimes in the open porch that I had to perform the most mundane of my assigned duties. I was the designated "fly chaser." I was equipped with a long pole with many streamers tied to one end. While the boarders were eating, I walked up and down, alongside the long dining table, waving my stick back and forth to chase the flies away.

Again, our mother was the heart, soul, and general manager of the entire operation. Also, she was probably the hardest worker in the family, working from dawn till dark, seven days a week. She did all of the cooking for all of the meals. In addition, she was a superb baker of bread, pies, strudels, and all sorts of bakery products. She, with my sisters, did all of the washing of the sheets, towels, and linens, by hand. I remember these Mondays vividly because it was my job to fill the three giant wash tubs with water. It took 26 pails of water which had to be carried up from the creek to fill the tubs. The "soft" water from the creek was ideal for laundry purposes. The two sisters did all of the interior work: fixing beds, keeping the house clean, chamber maid duties, ironing, waiting on tables, washing dishes, etc.. Feeding the chickens and collecting the eggs were also part of their duties.

My brother was lucky in that he had a summer job helping a fruit and vegetable peddler, Jack Fallon, sell his produce from an old Model "T" Ford truck to the nearby boarding houses. Probably, his most memorable incident was when the engine on the old truck misfired, while being cranked to get it started. The "kick back" of the crank knocked out one of his front teeth.

Big Joe was responsible for the outdoor activities. First and foremost, he dug, planted, weeded, and watered the large family garden. It provided almost all of the fresh vegetables needed for the boarding house. He built and maintained the long high retaining walls, which protected the property from erosion especially during floods. He built all of the outdoor benches, tables, furniture, and fences. Also, he built our large open porch, pig pen, chicken coop, smoke house, and grape arbors. The porch was used for summer dining and for recreational purposes during inclement weather.

One of his unique efforts was an 18 foot wooden rowboat. It was used for fishing and transporting people up, down, and across the creek. Probably, its most important use was to haul boatloads of fire wood for the house from the heavily forested areas upstream. All of the above were accomplished "by hand," without the benefit of any powered tools or devices.

As for myself, my primary duty at that stage was a "go-for" and minor assistant to Big Joe. Also each morning I had to walk to the village (about a half mile +) and pick up the mail. I also did the shopping in the village stores for whatever odds and ends were needed for the family or the boarders. Otherwise, I was continually at the side of Big Joe, helping as much as I was able; fetching and returning tools, nails, and boards; turning the large millstone for sharpening axes, knives, and scissors; and helping cut firewood for the stoves.

With the family organized and in place, the running of the boarding house proceeded quite smoothly. The following are some of my reminiscences of that period.

One of the events that comes to mind quite often is the picnic/ outing to Lake Mohonk. It was a beautiful resort area in the mountains, used almost exclusively by the very wealthy from New York City. It included a mile long, crystal clear lake nestled near the top of the highest mountain in the area. The trails, paths, and grounds were meticulously well kept, and even the forested areas had a manicured appearance. Wild life roamed the area freely.

Several times during the summer, the boarders hired a 12 passenger horse drawn shay to take them on a picnic/outing to Lake Mohonk. (see picture below)

Courtesy: Genero Family Collection

PICNIC/OUTING TO LAKE MOHONK: circa 1930

No motor vehicles were permitted on the mountain. Sometimes there was enough room in the shay to squeeze me in. After a fabulous picnic lunch, the boarders would explore the lake area and climb the bald face of the mountain to the pinnacle. There was a tower there, with a weather station and a forest ranger observation post. The view was magnificent, and on a clear day five different states were visible. After a full day of picnicking and mountain climbing, the boarders would climb aboard the horse drawn shay and return to Rosendale. It might be added that the tired and worn out returning group was in sharp contrast to the happy, singing, and frolicking group of the morning.

Whenever there was an extra large number of boarders (20-30) for a weekend, there would be an old fashioned open pit barbecue. Early Saturday morning, Big Joe would obtain a choice lamb from a local sheep ranch. By mid afternoon, it would be prepared, skewered on a spit about ten feet long and placed over a slow burning wood charcoal fire. There it would be slowly turned, basted, and roasted, until noon on Sunday. There was the problem of who would turn and baste the lamb throughout the night. Volunteers were obtained from the boarders. As an incentive, a bottle of our family's fine wine and some glasses were placed near the crank handle. After church on Sunday morning, the banquet type feast would begin.

As a footnote, sometimes the number of the boarders was so large that all of the beds in both the house and barn were occupied. On such an occasion, I would have pleasure of sleeping on the back seat of one of the large sedans owned by some of the more affluent boarders. My favorite was a "Reo Flying Cloud."

Of course the most enjoyable times were the afternoon swimming periods. After the noon meal, quiet was maintained to permit the boarders to enjoy their afternoon siestas. This was the time that I was free of all duties and could go swimming in the Rondout Creek. The village swimming hole was only about 200 yards upstream from our house. Since this was the era before air conditioners, the swimming hole was heavily used by the whole village. It was not unusual to have as many as 60 - 70 persons, all ages and sizes swimming in the creek on some of the warmer days. The swimming hole was almost ideal, It had modest beach areas; waist high wading areas, diving rocks, and a large 10 foot deep swimming hole in the middle. Some shore areas were shaded by very high trees. The one sunny area was a very large, smooth surface, rock outcropping. It was excellent for sun bathing and social gatherings.

Being a somewhat slow learner, I did not learn to swim until I was six years old. However, once I learned, it was difficult to keep me out of the water, rain or shine, hot or cold, low water or high water. I particularly enjoyed swimming after heavy rains, when the water in the creek would rise about 5 - 10 feet. Then a group of us teenagers would float on the swift currents down to the village. There, we could jump off the village bridge into the creek, because now the water was sufficiently high to do so safely.

The saddist part of these summers took place the week after Labor Day. It was then that we had to return to the city and go back to school.

The Great Depression:

As explained earlier, The adverse effects of the depression were not felt by the family until after 1933. Therefore, this section will focus on the latter half of the depression.

Because of the family homestead in Rosendale there never was a problem with food. There was always an abundant supply of tasty and nutritious food. The following is a summary of our food sources during that period.

Fruits and vegetables were grown on the homestead. The fruits were apples, pears, cherries, grapes, and quince. The latter fruit originated in China. It was not eaten directly, but made into an excellent jelly. The other fruits were either eaten directly, made into jellies, or preserved in glass jars. Our mother would make 100+ jars of jelly each year.

The garden provided most of the vegetables used by the family and boarders. The most popular items were cabbage, corn, kale, green peppers, beans, onions, carrots, lettuce, radishes, tomatoes, egg-plants, and pumpkins (which practically grew wild all over the place). As with the fruits, those that could not be consumed immediately, and could be cooked, were preserved in glass jars for later use. A pleasant memory for me was when I took a salt shaker into the garden, picked a ripe tomato, put salt on it, and consumed it on the spot. All other vegetables were usually obtained in bulk quantities from local farmers.

The family raised about 200+ chickens each year. Besides providing meat throughout the year, they produced so many eggs that, at times, the eggs were shipped in special egg crates to the rest of the family in the city.

Four to six pigs were raised in Rosendale each year. These provided the family not only with chops and roasts, but with our own smoked and cured bacon, hams, and sausages. Our prosciuttos were renown for their quality and tastiness. The pig's feet were used for soup and the pig's head with an apple in its mouth was served as a Christmas delicacy.

Our Friday (fish) meals were never a problem. The Rondout Creek teamed with fish. During the boarding season, it was customary for Big Joe and I to get up very early and walk about a mile up the creek. We would then wade in the creek slowly back to the house. Along the way, we would fish in all of the fishing holes. When we got home we would always have a mess of fish. Then we would clean them and have them ready for the noon and evening meals. The large ones were baked, and the smaller ones were used to make mother's delicious fish chowder. Even during winter months when the creek was frozen over, fresh fish were available. Off season, whenever a large fish was caught, it was quickly placed in the large water barrel in the well house. A small stream of well water ran constantly into the barrel. There, the fished thrived quite well. Whenever one was needed for a meal, we simply reached into the barrel and pulled one out.

The fall of the year was gourmet time. Wild game and fowl were plentiful. On occasion, Mother prepared "pheasant under glass" for the Sunday meal.

Then too, the fall of the year was also the time for some of our family's unique home made specialties. It was the time when the grapes were ripe and ready for making wine. It was our pride and joy. The family made 200+ gallons each year. It had a savory mellow taste, neither too harsh, nor too sweet. It was served at all meals and prized by all.

The grapes grown by our family were supplemented by choice grapes from nearby vineyards. Big Joe was an expert at selecting the best grapes, those on the proper side of the hill, with the right amount of sun, and just right for picking. The making of wine was relatively simple. First, the barrels had to be scrubbed thoroughly and water-aged in the creek properly. The grapes were mashed in large half-barrels. Yes, they were stomped by feet, albeit,wearing thoroughly scrubbed boots. When fermented, the wine was drained off and put into the cured barrels.

During the depression, it was common to make a "second" wine. Several pails of water and sugar were mixed with the residue of the "first" wine. They were then thoroughly mixed and left to ferment a "second" time. As with the "first" wine, it was drained off and put into barrels. When done properly, only a wine connoisseur could tell the difference.

Wine was available at all meals to all members of the family. The amount of water mixed with the wine was inversely related to the age of the person drinking the wine.

Perhaps, there was one more home made product which should be mentioned, rye whiskey. The family had a small copper still which was used to make "rye" whiskey. Our excellent fresh well water was poured into a couple barrels, which were about half filled with rye grain. Yeast was added and it was allowed to ferment. After fermentation, the liquid was cooked and the vapors run through our copper still. It was a slow process, and the end product was only about 15-20 gallons. Tested in a hydrometer, it registered 145 proof. Besides family use, it was an excellent bartering agent with the local farmers, especially when buying farm items in bulk, such as potatoes. Incidentally, the author still possesses a 70 year old pint sample of the last batch.

As can be seen from the foregoing, there never was a shortage of food for the table. However, a special mention should be made of our dear friend and grocer from nearby Tilson, the Keators. They were kind enough to let our family buy items on credit during the long winter months, delaying payment till the summer boarding house season.

A small but steady flow of hard cash was provided by the two oldest sisters working in the City. Occasionally, this was augmented by Big Joe in Rosendale. Because of his experience in tunneling, rock drilling, and blasting, he worked part time for the town's highway department. His specialty was blasting away sides of mountains and giant boulders, which were hindering road construction.

Of interest also is the fact that whenever possible, items were purchased in bulk quantities. As an example, flour and sugar were purchased in 100 pound bags. The sugar arrived with a bonus. The interior lining of the burlap bag was made of high quality cotton cloth. Mother would separate the cloth from the burlap. Then, she would the sew an edging around the cloth. This would result in an excellent dish towel, some of which are still in use, 70 years later.

The family survived the depression reasonably well by means of hard work, steadfast determination, wise use of resources, and careful control of their hard currency.

CHAPTER 4

TEEN-YEARS IN
NEW YORK CITY/ROSENDALE

Preface:

The nation was still deeply mired in a depression. The family remained split. Our parents were in Rosendale. The rest of us lived primarily in the City. However, we always spent the holidays together, usually in Rosendale.

This was the period of my senior teenage (14 - 18) years and covers my activities in both the City and Rosendale. For convenience, it will be divided into two parts:

De La Salle High School
Summers in Rosendale (Part 2)

De La Salle High School:

At this point, I would like to digress and mention my Guardian Angel. Too many unforeseen and beneficial things have happened to me throughout my lifetime to arrive at any other conclusion. Sometimes the effects were not immediately apparent, but generally, the long term effects were both significant and beneficial. This was the first "overt" example of such an instance.

After graduating from Saint Paul's grade school, I had assumed that I would be going to Commerce Public High School. It was where a large number of Saint Paul graduates went, and it was located just across the street from our apartment. My parents decided that somehow, they would find the money needed to send me to a Catholic high school. De La Salle was chosen. It was within walking distance and the closest to our apartment. Also, it saved subway fare. How my Guardian Angel influenced my parents to make this decision, I do not know. However, its beneficial effects helped shape my entire future life.

De La Salle was one of the most challenging Catholic high schools in the city. It was a small "prep" type school, with less than 200 students. It was a no-nonsense school run by the Christian Brothers. No time was wasted having the students change classrooms for different subjects. It was the Brothers who changed classes. Jackets and ties were required.

Lunch time was limited to only about 30 minutes. There was no cafeteria and no hot meals were served. They had several large folding tables in the gym, upon which were served prepared sandwiches, and some baked goods, as well as milk and soft drinks. Generally, the more affluent students bought their lunches. The rest of us students brought sandwiches from home. I was given 5 cents a day to buy a small container of milk to go with my meal. I must have eaten a thousand peanut butter and jelly sandwiches.

We were required to take four years of mathematics, history, English, a foreign language, and religion. I managed to earn an "honorable mention" in science. The only choice that I was given was in my senior year. I could take either Latin or French.

Studies were intense. Homework in every subject, every night was the norm, with a little extra for weekends and holidays. Student study periods were unknown. The Christian brothers maintained tight discipline. Slipshod or lackadaisical performance was not tolerated. I can not recall of having heard of a student who failed to pass the annual New York State regents examinations. When one graduated from De La Salle, one was prepared for both the challenges of higher education and the harsh realities of life in general.

No "school time off" was allowed for athletics. De La Salle did not have a baseball or football team. It did have a horse riding club, a modest basketball team, and a renowned track and field team. It had a national champion one mile relay team. John Quigley, the anchor of the relay team, was considered to be the fastest quarter mile sprinter on the East Coast, if not in the nation. He was given a scholarship to Manhattan College and was being groomed for the 1940 Olympics (cancelled because of WW II).

As for myself, I tried out for the track team. I managed to earn a few awards during my three years on the team, see below. However, I never earned enough points in intercity competition during a single year to be awarded a school letter.

MEDALS/AWARDS WON AT DE LA SALLE

Photograph - Genero Family Collection

I finally did manage to earn a school letter in my senior year by becoming manager of the basketball team. Basically, my duties were to be the score keeper and/or time keeper during the official games. Probably, my most important function was to carry the team's basketballs on crowded subways, to and from the games and practice sessions.

An interesting feature about attending high school at De La Salle, was that few, if any, lasting personal relationships were formed during those four years. The students came from all parts of the city. The tendency was for the students to return to their neighborhoods and continue their existing relationships. This fulfilled their social and recreational needs. For me, it meant a return to the community at Saint Paul's.

At Saint Paul's Church, we continued to serve at scheduled masses and other religious services. We were now considered old enough to help with the parish bingo games. To earn spending money, I sold the *Catholic News* after masses on Sundays. Our recreational activities centered around 60th Street and on occasion, in Central Park. Our gathering place was Broker's Ice Cream Parlor, next to the church.

Probably our most enjoyable events during this period were our visits to the old ROXY theater, just a few blocks from Times Square. Until the opening of Radio City Music Hall, it was the largest movie theater in New York City. On Sundays, they had a 25 cents special for teenagers, if they purchased their tickets before 1 PM. Although this gave us admission to the theater, we usually had to wait in line inside the theater for about a half hour before seats became available. Our seats were in the top balcony, in the most remote areas of this giant theater. The wait was well worth it. We got to see the first run of top rated movies. In addition, there was a newsreel, a travel feature, and a short comedy. Most important of all, there were five acts of live vaudeville, featuring some of the top entertainers in the country. The entire performance would last 3 to 4 hours. It made for a very pleasant and comfortable Sunday afternoon.

As may be noted, life during this period was quite routine. Nothing spectacular took place to gain our attention, or interfere with our lives. We were in that transitional period of our lives. We were preparing to assume our responsibilities and to cope with the challenges of the future. For me De La Salle was the key ingredient in that preparation.

Summers in Rosendale (Part 2):

In general things continued pretty much as before. I was still the "go for"member of the family. However, there was one significant improvement. I now had a nice new bicycle. I could complete my trips to the village much more quickly. Also, when I was working with Big Joe, I was becoming a more effective helper.

It was during this period that I had my first job. Our Deputy Sheriff needed an assistant, and I was hired. He was assigned to protect a road construction site and associated equipment in the nearby mountains. The problem was that it was a 12 hour shift, 6 PM to 6 AM. I was to accompany the Deputy Sheriff during this period and report anything unusual that I saw or heard. My real job was to keep the Deputy Sheriff company so that he would not doze during that period. Sometimes, I would lose the battle with the comfortable seat cushions in his car and become drowsy. Later, around 6 AM, I would wake up with a start. My pay was 25 cents a night.

Another thing that I did to earn "pin" money during the summer was to sell dobsons (hellgramites); 5 cents each, to visiting fishermen from the city. The dobson was the best live fishing bait for the large mouth bass, which inhabited the lakes and streams in the area.

The nesting place for the dobson was under rocks in swift flowing water, as in rapids. The general rule was that the bigger the rock, the bigger and more numerous the dobsons. Big Joe and I worked together. He would lift the big rocks, and I would catch the dobsons. Sometimes a fair sized water snake would object to our disturbing his domicile. Big Joe had the simple solution. He would drop the rock back on top of the snake.

Probably, the most notable event that occurred during this period concerned Jack Fallon, my brother's employer. It all began when I was swimming down Rondout Creek.

Occasionally, we better swimmers would go about a half mile up the creek to an area called "the rapids." The rapids were swift flowing and a little notorious. Actually, the rapids were ancient sluice ways, which were used to turn giant water wheels. These turned the large, heavy millstones which were used to grind limestone clinker into natural cement. Going through the rapids was definitely not for beginners. After having our fun, we would swim back downstream to our swimming hole.

One Sunday afternoon, while we were swimming in a quiet stretch of water back to our swimming hole, I noticed a fisherman on the bank. Instead of fishing, apparently he was sleeping peacefully.

As it was getting dark that evening, Jack Fallon's wife and a search party were going along the creek near our house, looking for her husband. Upon hearing this, I told them that I had seen a fisherman sleeping on the banks of the creek. I led them to the spot and we climbed down the steep embankment. He was still there in the same position. However, he was not sleeping. Weighing almost 300 pounds, the climb down the steep embankment apparently was just too strenuous for him. He had suffered a fatal heart attack. It was the only time that my name ever appeared in the Rosendale News.

One final comment about our swimming hole. It seemed that as the boys and girls got older, they spent less time swimming. They began spending more time on the smooth high rocks, sunning and socializing, (see picture next page):

Courtesy: Genero Family Collection
ROSENDALE SWIMMING HOLE: CIRA1948

The summer of 1938, was to be my last summer assisting the family with their boarding house activities. I would be graduating high school the following year. Then I was expected to go out, get a job and help support the family.

To finish the summer in grand style, I had planned to attend the gala celebration and dance at the end of the village. It was being held on Saturday evening, Labor Day weekend. To prepare for it, I got all slicked up in my white duck trousers and white sport shirt. About 8 PM, I headed to the village for the celebration.

Background: This was the year that I became a volunteer fireman. It was before Fire/Rescue, and any one who was available automatically became a volunteer fireman. The Rosendale fire truck had been a 1916 Ford Model T truck. It was painted red, carried a few lengths of hose, a couple of ladders, and a large number of pails (to form a bucket brigade). In order to get it started, the volunteers literally pushed the engine out onto the road; then they pushed it down the street as fast as they could until its engine started. Once started, it ran fine. This all changed in August 1938. The village bought a brand new Ford V-8 fire engine, with an integrated water pumping capability. It was the most modern fire engine in the county. Often the driver would collect a few of us volunteer teenagers and go to the creek to test the water pumping capability of the fire engine. Us teenagers were needed to unload, drag, and then reload the hoses.

Back to Saturday night, Labor Day weekend. Just as I was walking past the fire house, the fire alarm sounded. I and others immediately ran to the fire house, and climbed aboard the new fire engine. The fire was at the Half-Moon dairy farm about three miles away. The fire engines that were already on the scene did not have a water pumping capability. We were to be their salvation. The first dairy barn was already ablaze.

The plan was for us to hose down the second barn in order to keep it from catching fire. The engine went to a nearby stream, and we stretched out the entire 500 feet of hose. As the second barn was beginning to catch fire, there still was no water coming out of our hose. After about 15 minutes, I went down to the engine to see what was the problem.

The engine was by the stream. The suction hose was in the water, and the motor of the fire engine was turning over as fast as it could. As luck would have it, the experienced driver was out of town and the substitute driver did not know how to engage the pump. There were three or four men there, holding flashlights, trying to read the book of instructions. They kept turning valves, engaging levers and racing the engine, trying to figure out how to get the suction pump working. In the mean time, the second barn had caught fire. Luckily, they finally hit the correct combination and we were able to save the third barn. After pulling hoses and sloshing around in the dairy farm "muck", we were no longer very clean, nor odor free. When we returned to the village, the celebration was over. In any event, we were not in fit condition to go to a dance. On returning home, I spent some time scrubbing to become sufficiently clean so that I could go to bed.

So went my final night of celebrating my last summer weekend in Rosendale.

CHAPTER - 5

POST - TEEN YEARS IN NEW YORK CITY

Preface:

This chapter covers the two year period after high school and before entering military service. It was a period during which I was trying to define my future and decide upon an appropriate career. The country was still in a deep depression and World War II in Europe was just beginning.

Although jobs were scarce, I never was without a job for more than two weeks. My first priority was to get a job, regardless of the type, or salary. As can be seen, I tried a number of approaches, before my Guardian Angel quietly slipped in, and started me in the right direction.

R. H. Macys
Strauss Eckardt
Sherinhide
New York Central Railroad
Social Activities

R. H. Macy's:

During the Summer of 1939, after graduation from high school, I obtained a temporary job with the New York Central Railroad (more details later). When the job terminated at the end of the summer, it was just in time for another seasonal job. The department stores had begun hiring to meet their needs for the Christmas shopping season.

I was hired as a stock clerk by R. H. Macy's. Specifically, I was a merchandise price marker in the shoe department. There were thousands of pairs of shoes, both on the sale's floor and in the adjacent warehouse. My job was to ensure that the price marked on each shoe was correct. Each morning I was given very lengthy listing of shoe stock numbers and the correct price for that day (sales, specials, etc.). I would then locate the shoe, check the price on the shoe, and change the price if necessary. There was little problem with the shoes on the sales floor. However, the shoes in the warehouse were a different matter.

The shoes were stacked in steel storage bins from floor to ceiling (14 feet high). Sometimes, in the late afternoon, when working in the top bins, I would become drowsy. One afternoon, the supervisor discovered me in the top bin being a little too drowsy. The next day, I was transferred to a different section, which was a little more visible to the supervisor. Needless to say, when the Christmas season was over, I was not asked to stay on as a permanent employee.

For me, there was one strange requirement for Macy's male employees. We were required to wear a jacket and hat when coming to work. Normally, I never wore a hat. This rule was intended to reduce pilferage. Men could not come to work without a hat and jacket, because when going home, they might simply take one off a rack, and walk out as if it was their personal property.

When I left R. H. Macy's, I left with the firm belief that in 1939, Macy's handled only quality products and that they were sold at a fair price.

Strauss - Eckardt :

Strauss - Eckardt was a fair sized company that imported sundries, such as toys, ceramics, Christmas ornaments, and hardware items.

It also had factories in Europe and in the United States, which made similar items. Its customers were chain stores, department stores, and 5 & 10 cents stores.

The company had a job opening for a messenger/office boy. Three of us were interviewed for the job. The other two applicants seemed to embellish their qualifications by claiming that they were going to night school to further their education. Listening to my guardian angel, I simply told the truth. No, I was not going to night school. I got the job. It seemed that occasionally the job required night work.

The office portion of the job was quite simple: distributing the mail, handling office supplies, etc. However, I thought that I was going to be fired after only a few days on the job. A very important air mail letter that I had hand carried to the Post Office was returned because of insufficient postage. To prevent this from happening again, I would arrive at the office a half hour early and sort the mail, looking for returned letters. There never was another letter returned because of incorrect postage.

The messenger part of the job was the most interesting. I learned how to use every means of public transportation in the city and how to pin point the location of any given address. I handled bank deposits and delivered our company's certified checks. I cleared shipping documents through US Customs and delivered them to the various shipping companies. In addition, there was a constant flow of letters, invoices, and promotional materials that had to be delivered to potential customers and the company's own factories located in the metropolitan area.

My most interesting trip was to the owner's estate in Mamaroneck, NY, an exclusive suburb of New York City. He was home ill, and there were some important papers that required his immediate signature. I was sent to his estate with the papers. I was met at the railroad station and driven to his estate in a chauffer driven big black limousine. The building was enormous and the grounds were manicured to perfection. I was ushered into his very large bedroom, which alone was larger than the entire four room apartment in which I lived. It was my first glimpse into how the wealthy lived.

One of my less pleasant messenger trips was to the Holland-American Steamship Company. Strauss-Eckardt had a large harmonica factory in Holland (the United States did not produce quality harmonicas). There were about 100,000 of our harmonicas in crates sitting on the docks of Rotterdam. Weeks were spent obtaining the necessary clearance from the British government to have them shipped to the United States through the British blockade. We finally obtained the required clearance, and I took the papers to the office of the Holland-American steamship company. Two days later, Germany invaded Holland. They bombed and destroyed the dock/warehouse area, along with our 100,000 harmonicas.

Probably my most pleasant messenger service was unofficial. I had to spend a significant amount of time in our packing and shipping department in an adjacent warehouse. There, the shipping crew enjoyed a mid-afternoon brew. They made a special box into which they placed their half gallon growler. I would take the box and go down the freight elevator to the nearby tavern. I would hand the box to the bartender and tell him that it was for Otto. He would fill the growler with beer. I would carry it carefully back up the freight elevator to Otto. Sometimes he rewarded me by letting me have the first sip.

Strauss-Eckardt was located on 17th Street, across the street from Union Square. Occasionally, if it was a pleasant day, I would have my lunch in the park. At that time, Union Square was an outlet for every radical element of that era. Every day, there would be a dozen or so speakers on their little portable stands, shouting as loudly as possible in support of their specific cause. It was a little surprising to see them prominently displaying their American flag, while praising the Soviet Union.

When summer approached, I left Strauss-Eckardt and went back to my temporary job working for the railroad.

New York Central Railroad:

In June, I went to work for the New York Central Railroad as a temporary employee, for the second year. My job was that of a baggage handler and a relief ticket collector.

Historical Background: Except for Penn Station and Grand Central Station in Manhattan, all of the smaller railroads had their New York City terminals in New Jersey. The passengers rode ferry boats to cross the Hudson River to the city. The New York Ontario & Western (Erie) Railroad, and the West Shore (New York Central) Railroad had their joint terminal in Weehawken, New Jersey. It was a short covered walk from the trains to the ferries. The ferries (New York Central) had two terminals in Manhattan. One Manhattan terminal was directly across the river at 42d Street. The other terminal was down at the tip of Manhattan, at Cortlandt Street. I worked at the Cortlandt Street terminal. Later, it was the site of the World Trade Center.

The job of baggage handler was not quite as easy a job as it might seem. Railroad passengers checked their baggage through to their destinations in much the same manner as is done with airlines today. There were a couple of differences. In those days, there were no power driven conveyor systems as at the airports today. All baggage was handled manually, and there were no weight restrictions. It was common for passengers to ship their belongings in trunks, some weighing 150+ pounds. It might be added that some of the bags that were checked were in a very dilapidated condition. They bore a greater resemblance to a few pieces of cardboard, lashed together with a short piece of rope, than they did to a suitcase.

Things got quite busy during the summer months especially for the baggage handler. Literally, thousands of kids were shipped from the city to summer camps in the Catskill Mountains.
Their most common item of baggage was a foot locker, weighing 50 to 100 pounds. Many times, the footlockers would arrive at the terminal by the truck load.

The reasons for wanting to work for the railroad were many. The depression years were still not over. The pay was quite good, considered to be a comfortable "living wage" at that time. Chances for advancement were excellent. The job was fully protected by the powerful Brotherhood of Railroad Worker's Union. Probably the most important incentive was the excellent retirement system, fully guaranteed by the United States government. Once a person was on board as a "permanent" employee, he was set for life.

By the end of my second summer, I had worked my way up the ladder to number one on the waiting list for "permanent" employment. It usually took a family connection to get on to the waiting list. My connection was Uncle Fred.

As can be surmised, the job was very routine and not very challenging. Hardly anything of an exciting nature ever happened. I can recall only one event that was a little out of the ordinary.

One day, a female passenger came to the baggage room and complained bitterly about the condition in which her bag arrived at her destination. When she picked it up at her destination, many of her garments and undergarments were covered with black axel grease. Nothing much came of the complaint, since she was partly at fault. She had packed her bag in a very slovenly manner. She had made little, or no attempt to insure that all of her clothes were "inside" her bag. Much of her clothing was hanging out the sides of her bag. Later, I heard from one of the very senior tenured employees that maybe the axel grease did not soil her clothes accidentally.

Sherinhide:

As happened the previous year, the termination of my temporary employment with the railroad coincided with the beginning of the Christmas shopping season. The Sherinhide Company needed someone to manage its stock room and to do packaging and shipping. I applied for the job. The manner in which I was hired was interesting.

Sherinhide was a major producer of industrial leather belting. Sensing that the demand for leather belting was declining, management tried to diverse its product lines with other leather products. The company made beautifully laminated leather humidors, cigarette boxes, ashtrays, and jewelry boxes. The products were expensive and handled only by top of the line department stores and gift shops.

This is where my previous sojourns into the Strauss Eckardt shipping warehouse became beneficial. The packaging and shipping crew there taught me the basics of the tasks involved. In those days all cardboard boxes packed for shipping were required to be bound with twine or rope, in addition to the gummed sealing tape. The packaging crew taught me an intricate but rapid method of tying such boxes. The twine could be pulled tight for a snug fit and the knots had an effective "non slip" characteristic.

When I applied for the job at Sheirnhide, the manager arranged a test for me. He pointed to a number of items and instructed me to pack them and get the box ready for shipment. I packed the box quickly and readied it for shipment. The manager was so amazed when he saw the manner in which I tied the box with twine that he hired me on the spot.

The work was quite routine and nothing exciting took place. As Christmas season was approaching, the factory became very busy, and the company had to hire more workers. I went to our old Saint Paul's neighborhood and found three of my buddies who were still unemployed. Sherinhide hired all three for the Christmas season. An interesting situation arose on their first payday.

On their way home, they stopped at a local tavern and decided to celebrate with a couple of beers. One of them was refused service after the first beer. The bartender thought that he was intoxicated.

The next day we solved the problem. He had worked all day in the leather cleaning department. There, they used the trichlorethylene process to clean the leather. One of the solvents used was carbon tectrachloride. Prolonged exposure to the fumes of "carbontec" would give the person a slight "buzz." When mixed with a little alcohol, it could cause a person to appear intoxicated.

After Christmas, business slowed appreciably. A question arose as to whether there was further need for a full time packer and shipper. It was another instance in my life when I received a little help from above to help guide my future. This will be explained more fully in the next section.

There was one non-work related incident, which took place during the holidays and may be worthy of note. Christmas afternoon, I walked through the old neighborhood and past the Henry Hudson Hotel. The hotel was an upscale women's residential hotel. It had an outdoor canopy and a uniformed doorman. On each side of the entrance, there was a beautifully shaped and potted cedar/ Christmas tree. This day there was only one tree and the short stump of the second tree in the other pot.

It seems that there was one very poor family in the neighborhood. That year, they could not even afford a Christmas tree. The five children all went to bed Christmas Eve with tears in their eyes. As Santa was passing over that night, he noticed the plight of the family. He also noticed the Henry Hudson Hotel with the potted Christmas trees at the entrance. Having a hand saw in his sleigh, he stopped. He cut down one of the trees and delivered it to the needy family. Christmas morning, that family had five of the happiest children in the city.

Social Activities:

It was interesting to note that there was a gradual shift in our interests during this period. Less time was being spent on street games and more time was being spent trying to get along with the young ladies.

World War II had just begun in Europe. The United States declared that it was a neutral nation. Although our national economy was improving, about half of our crowd was still not fully employed. I was one of the more fortunate ones. Now that I was working, our family could afford to move to a more pleasant neighborhood; Woodside, Long Island. However, my social activities remained centered around my old friends at Saint Paul's.

Broker's Ice Cream Parlor, next to the church, was still our meeting place. Since I was normally working full-time, my involvement was limited to Saturday evenings and Sunday afternoons. It should be mentioned that the legal drinking age in New York was eighteen. Therefore, occasionally a few of us dropped in to one of the local taverns for a beer or two.

Sunday afternoon was an example of a shift in our interests. Weather permitting, it was not unusual for a mixed group of us to go for a walk in Central Park. We cheered for our neighborhood baseball team, fed the squirrels, went for row boat rides on the lake, or went to the zoo. We would take our little Brownie Box Cameras with us and take a few pictures. When the weather was bad, we went to the movies.

Our major activity during this period was the Saturday night dance. Every Saturday there would be a dance in the parish social hall. Admission was 15 cents and there were usually between 50 to 75 at the dance. The music was recorded. We could dance or just listen to recordings of the most popular bands of that time such as Glen Miller, Artie Shaw, and Tommy Dorsey. Frank Sinatra was the idol of that period.

Periodically there would be a really big dance in the basement auditorium of the church featuring a live band, which would attract anywhere from 200-300 of us.

I once asked Father Ward, the parish coordinator for these events, why the church spent so much time sponsoring dances. He replied that is was good for young boys and girls to associate with each other in a healthy church related environment. A little later he confided that maybe the boys and girls would become better acquainted and form closer relationships, resulting in marriages and the raising of families within the church.

Later, I realized how forward thinking the church was. It was at one of these dances that I met the very attractive and vivacious Betty Myers, the future Mrs. Genero.

There were also dances in Rosendale, but of a different variety, i.e. "country dances." The last one that I attended before entering the service was sponsored by the Rosendale Grange. The Grange was a national farm organization established for social and political purposes.

The dance was held in the Rosendale Grange Hall and attendance was about 100. Along one side of the hall was a long table filled with baskets of food, cakes, pies and other assorted goodies, all prepared by the local farm wives. The Rosendale Ginger-Snaps provided the music with fiddle, banjo, piano and drums.

Near the end of the evening at one of these dances, I finally got up enough courage to ask the prettiest girl in the village for a dance. She had just been elected the Ulster County Apple Blossom Queen. I didn't realize that it was a "change partners" dance. We danced about 6 steps when the whistle blew, and she was swept away by scores of other men who were waiting for an opportunity to dance with her.

Things did not get any better. Later, during a square dance, all the men were dancing in a line on one side of the hall. The women were in a similar line on the opposite side. At the call "Shake your partner," the men were supposed to cross to the other side, grab their partner, swing her around, then dance (stomp) back to the men's line. On one such call, my partner happened to be the biggest and most powerful farm wife in Rosendale. She literally picked me up till my feet were off the floor, spun me around, then set me down so I could dance back to the men's line. She was thoroughly enjoying herself and laughing heartily all of the time. It was five years before I went to another dance in Rosendale.

It was at one of the church dances in the city that events unfolded which changed my life dramatically. One evening before Christmas, 1940, a couple of us stopped at one of the local taverns to have a beer before going home. Johnny, a silvered tongued Irishman, was in our group. He explained that there was a once in a lifetime opportunity for all of us young men to go on a one year vacation and get paid for it.

The United States had officially declared itself a "neutral nation" regarding the war in Europe. However, it was deemed prudent to strengthen our military. Congress authorized the President to call the National Guard to active duty for one year of intensive training. What made the situation attractive to us was that there was a National Guard armory only two blocks away on 62nd Street. As a group, we could all join the 212th Regiment stationed there. We could all be in the same battery and have fun together for a whole year while drawing full army pay. This would have the additional benefit of all of us remaining together and looking out for each other. If we waited to be drafted, we would be just another number in a vast pool of strangers. Ten of us took advantage of Johnny's proposal.

As for myself, the timing was perfect. My job at Sherinhide was winding down and there was still not an opening for a permanent job with the railroad. That opening did not happen until three months after our regiment was activated, and we were in our training camp in Georgia. By then it was too late and my future course was set. Throughout my life, it seems to me there was an unseen hand guiding my fate.

Our regiment was called to active duty in February 1941. We marched out of the armory, down 9th Avenue to the Pennsylvania Railroad Station. There we boarded a troop train that took us to our training camp in Georgia. As we marched down 9th Avenue, the sidewalks were lined with thousands of people cheering and waving us on. One of the bystanders waving us on was Johnny the silver tongued Irishman. He had failed to pass the Army physical exam (hernia).

CHAPTER 6

UNITED STATES ARMY (Enlisted Status)

Preface:

The 212th New York National Guard Regiment was a "Coast Artillery" Regiment. Previously it had been the 12th Infantry Regiment of Civil War fame. After World War I, the importance of antiaircraft fire was recognized, and as a result it was re-organized into a "Coast Artillery" Antiaircraft Regiment. The rational for antiaircraft being assigned to Coast Artillery rather than Field Artillery, was that Coast Artillery fired at moving targets, while Field Artillery fired at stationary targets. This was corrected during the Korean War when all artillery was combined into a single Artillery Branch.

When federalized in February 1941, the regiment had three primary weapon systems: 1, Automatic Weapons (50 caliber machine guns and 37mm rapid fire cannons); 2, heavy antiaircraft weapons (3" high velocity cannons); and 3, Searchlights. All 10 of us from the Saint Paul's neighborhood were assigned to the searchlight battery, commonly referred to as "moonlight cavalry."

This was before the era of precision radars, and antiaircraft gunners had to visually see the target before they could open fire. The searchlights were used to illuminate the targets at night, so that they could be engaged by antiaircraft weapons.

The searchlights were 60 inches in diameter, had 1,000,000 candle power, and were ignited by the contact of large carbon electrodes. They were directed to targets by two large audio horns (elephant ears) for angle of elevation, and two horns for horizontal direction. The horns were mounted an a large pedestal type of trailer and could be turned or elevated to search for targets, see photo.

The operators were connected to the horns by an audio system. They listened for the sound of an aircraft engine. When the sound to both ears was equalized, they would shout "on target." The searchlight, which was synchronized with the horns, would then be turned on, and the operators would begin to visually search for the aircraft.

Were sound locators effective? On one occasion when both listeners shouted "on target", the searchlight was turned on and it illuminated a passing freight train.

Courtesy: Fort MacArthur Museum, San Pedro, CA

60" SEARCHLIGHT - CONTROL STATION, WITH NIGHT BINOCULARS - AUDIO HORNS (ELEPHANT EARS)

By the end of the war, antiaircraft units were equipped with heavier guns (90mm), new rapid fire cannons (40mm), and newly developed very accurate radars. One radar was so tiny that they could fit it into the nose of an artillery shell. It exploded the shell when it was in close proximity to an airplane.

Before Pearl Harbor
After Pearl Harbor
Three Musheteers from Saint Paul's

Before Pearl Harbor:

We arrived at Camp Stewart, about 40 miles from Savannah, in late February 1941. We lived in pyramidal tents, six per tent, with a small coal burning heater in the center for cold nights. The tents were stretched over wood frames, which helped considerably.

I was looking forward to begin training, but there were other tasks which had priority, see photo below:

DIGGING DEEP
DRAINAGE DITCHES
CAMP STEWART, GA

(AUTHOR IN FORGROUND)

Courtesy: Genero Family Collection

Initially, I was assigned to the communications section as a telephone lineman. Since our searchlights were deployed in a checkerboard pattern over an area 10 miles square, good reliable communications were essential. The hours were long and the job was not without its hazards. We lost one of our crew members during maneuvers. He fell off a high pole.

I was not a good pole climber, so I gravitated towards driving the truck for the communications section. This was interesting since I did not have a civilian driver's license, and I did not know how to drive.

The personnel of the 212th Regiment came from the less affluent lower Westside of Manhattan. As a result, virtually no one owned an automobile and very few had a driver's license. Since the 212th was a mobile regiment, a major program was instituted to teach the members how to drive. I applied immediately. Within a couple of weeks, I passed the test and was issued my Army driver's license.

I was quite content with driving the small Chevrolet 1-1/2 ton telephone maintenance truck. All of this changed during the summer of 1941. Our battery was one of the first units in the US Army to be issued one of the newly invented Signal Corps radars (photo below). They had a range of only about 25 miles, but they were infinitely better than the audio sound systems, which we had been using.

Courtesy: Army Communications - Electronics Museum, Fort Monmouth, NJ

SIGNAL CORPS RADAR - SCR-268

As for me, the most important items of issue with these radars were the 20 large prime-movers used to move them. A prime-mover was an extra large cargo truck that could also tow a large trailer. Because of its 10 wheel drive, it could operate effectively in rough terrain, as well as on highways.

It was one of the happiest days of my young life when I was assigned to drive one of these trucks. I was no longer a $21 a month recruit, but I was now a Private First Class, holding a very responsible position, see photo. Probably one of the main reasons that I was assigned one of these new trucks was that I kept my vehicle spotlessly clean and always ready for inspection. My buddies in the motor pool appreciated that.

Courtesy: Genero Family Collection
AUTHOR DRIVING PRIME MOVER

Since this was such an important event in my young life, it is believed that further elaboration is needed. Driving a prime-mover in 1941 was quite different from driving a big truck today.

There was no power-steering. The front wheels could not be

turned unless the vehicle was in motion. In order to give the driver leverage, the steering wheel was large, about 3 feet in diameter. It was attached to a steering post, which came up vertically through the floor of the cab and sat in the driver's lap.

This was the era before synchro-mesh transmissions. Double-clutching had to be done properly or there would be a loud clashing of gears and a significant reduction in speed until the gears could be engaged properly. There were 10 speeds forward and two in reverse. The tachometer (engine rpm) was more important than the speedometer. It told the driver when to shift gears. The trucks were equipped with governors, so that they could not exceed 38 miles per hour.

There were no Interstate expressways. Some bridges in the South were so narrow, that two trucks could not pass each other going in opposite directions. One would have to pull over on the shoulder of the road and wait for the other to cross over the bridge.

Two separate braking systems with separate controls were used, airbrakes for the truck and electric brakes for the trailers. Improper application of the brakes could cause the trailer to jack-knife, with possible serious consequences.

Driving these trucks was considered so important that each driver was given his individual set of keys. No one could drive my truck without my OK.

My prime-mover suffered a mishap while we were on maneuvers in Carolina. On a country dirt road, it was attacked by a persimmons tree. Soft, squashy persimmons rained all over my truck. It took a couple of days to scrape off the residue and make the truck presentable again.

During the summer, I was given a week's furlough and I visited my family in Rosendale. I told them proudly of my new job and my new responsibilities. Big Joe proudly showed me his latest accomplishment. He had the house connected to the town water supply system. For the first time, there was running water in the house. He proudly showed me the nice new bathroom, complete with bathtub and shower. Then he quietly told me that the bath room was for "guests." I was still expected to use the outdoor facilities.

I returned to my unit, which was still on maneuvers. Our searchlight was deployed in the middle of a poor farmer's cotton field. The farmer was cordial and even drew cool clear water out of his deep well for us. One day I was driving my prime-mover down a lonely country road. I saw the farmer walking down the same road carrying a heavy burlap sack. I stopped and gave him a lift. He was going down the road another couple miles to deliver the sack to a neighbor.

Later, being quite pleased with my charitable act, I related the incident to my buddies. Some of the older hands took me aside and acquainted me with "the facts of life." The cotton farmer had an illegal still and made moonshine. He stored it in jugs, which were hung on a long rope in his deep well. They told me that if I had been caught delivering moonshine, it would have meant 2 years in a federal penitentiary, with probably an extra year for using an Army truck to make the delivery. Needless to say, the farmer had to walk to make his future deliveries.

At the end of our three months of maneuvers in Georgia and the Carolinas, we returned to Camp Stewart. I was a few days late because I had to help deliver a radar to Fort Moultrie in Charleston, South Carolina. It was where the Civil War began. When we returned to Camp Stewart, it was dark and too late to unload the trucks. We just parked our trucks in the motor pool and went to our tents. We took showers, had a bite to eat, and then stretched out on our cots for a well earned rest. It was Saturday night, December 6th, 1941.

After Pearl Harbor:

After going to church Sunday morning, December 7th, I decided to walk to Hinesville, a town near Camp Stewart. I wanted to check on train schedules for the holiday season. While walking by a number of regimental areas on the post, I noticed large groups of soldiers gathered around some of the tents, i.e., those which had portable radios. Being curious, I stopped by one of the tents to find out what was holding their attention. After listening to the broadcasts, I decided that it would be a waste of time to go to Hinesville.

I returned to our battery area, and we spent the rest of the day speculating on what would be our nation's response to Pearl Harbor. We had no idea as to the true extent of the losses suffered. The official reports were that we had suffered minimal losses and only three small ships had been damaged or sunk. Our guesses ranged from the sending of a note of protest to Japan to a full declaration of war. To help us with our analysis of the situation, we all chipped in and hired a taxi to go to the next county for a bottle of bourbon. We were all restricted to camp, and Hinesville was in a "dry" county. That night none of us slept soundly.

The next morning, the entire regiment was marched out on to the parade grounds. Loud speakers were set up so we could hear the President's speech. By the time we marched back to our battery area, war had been declared, and we had been given our marching orders.

Our Battery was to proceed with the highest priority to Los Angeles. We were one of the few units in the United States Army that was equipped and trained with the new radars. Los Angeles was most important to our war effort, since it was the center of our nation's aviation industry (Douglas, North American, Lockheed, etc.). Coincidentally, all of the major Hollywood film studios were also located there, which helped with troop morale.

Flat cars had already been assembled at the camp's railroad yards, and we began loading immediately. My prime-mover had not been unloaded, so it was loaded on to a railroad flat car, as it was. We worked all through the night, and by dawn the next morning we were on our way.

It took us five days to reach Los Angeles. Traveling across the southern United States in the winter was a dull and dreary experience. There was little or no green vegetation. Everything appeared to be brown or covered with sand, rocks, and in a semi-desert status. This all changed when we arrived in California. Descending into the San Bernardino Valley was one of the most beautiful sights that I had ever seen. Everything was neat and green. The air was filled with the fragrance of orange blossoms. I felt that I was in heaven.

Upon arrival in Los Angeles, we were deployed immediately. All the searchlight units were spread , checkerboard fashion, from Santa Monica to Long Beach, and from the ocean, inland to Pasadena. Our radar equipped searchlights were stationed along the coastal areas, while those without radars were located further inland.

One of the saddest events that took place in California, during the early days of the war, was the internment of Japanese residents. They were herded, sometimes not too gently, into internment camps away from the coast. The excuse given was that they might be spies for Japan.

Most of the Japanese in the Los Angeles area were small shop owners or farmers. Their farms were of the "garden" variety. They were the most beautifully maintained, most productive, and most profitable in the area. I sometimes wondered if jealousy and a desire to covet their farms were not factors in aiding to reach this decision.

However, the order to intern the Japanese had one unintended beneficial effect. It saved many Japanese residents from bodily harm. There was an intense hatred among the local population against the Japanese. I even heard one serviceman brag about how he had fired a few rounds in their direction just for the fun of it.

Until the Battle of Midway, June 4 - 7, 1942, we took our duty of defending Los Angeles against a Japanese attack, quite seriously. The photograph of the author on the cover was taken during that period. I was on guard duty, protecting our radar/searchlight site adjacent to the Douglas Aircraft Factory in Santa Monica. The most memorable event during that period was the "Great Air Attack" on Los Angeles, February 25th, 1942. The sequence of events was as follows.

On the night of February 23-24, a Japanese submarine surfaced and fired a few rounds at the oil facilities in Santa Barbara (North of Los Angeles). No appreciable damage resulted. The submarine was last reported heading south towards Los Angeles.

On the night of February 24 -25, a long range radar in Los Angles reported an unidentified aircraft about 70 miles out to sea. The entire Los Angles area was put on maximum alert.

At about 3 AM, one of our searchlight crews visually sighted a moving light in the sky. They illuminated the object and identified it as a balloon with a flare attached to it. They turned off their light and reported it to the air defense operations center. The duty officer at the center ordered all lights to go into action and illuminate the balloon. All of our lights within range, illuminated the balloon. As soon as a number of lights illuminated the balloon, a massive antiaircraft barrage began. Thousands of antiaircraft rounds were fired at the intersection of the searchlight beams, see picture next page.

Courtesy: Los Angeles Times

SEARCHLIGHTS AND ANTIAIRCRAFT FIRE - LOS ANGELES, FEBRUARY 25, 1942

I was operating our radar and could not find any radar echo returning from that intersection. With the aid of a mechanical sight, I personally pointed the radar antenna exactly at the object, and still there was no radar return echo. Puzzled, I called over to Charlie at our control station and asked what was in the intersection of the searchlight beams. He reported that it was a balloon with a flare attached.

Not being satisfied, I went over to the control station, which was equipped with the finest night binoculars made in America. Clearly, the target was a balloon, about 10 feet in diameter, with an illuminated flare dangling from it. It was about 10,000 feet high, and the upper winds were carrying it out to sea and back. Firing continued until about 4 AM.

The antiaircraft units around the Douglas Aircraft Factory in Santa Monica did not open fire. It was their metrological balloon. At that time, antiaircraft gun units released metrological balloons into the atmosphere every six hours. Its purpose was to measure the winds aloft. Then they could adjust their antiaircraft fire to compensate for the wind direction and speed. At night, they would attach a flare to the balloon so that it could be tracked visually.

By some strange coincidence, the first two antiaircraft units from the Los Angeles area to be sent overseas were the regiment which sent the balloon aloft and our searchlight battalion, which illuminated the balloon.

The official response from Washington was that the guns were firing at unidentified aircraft. The numbers ranged from 1 to 15 aircraft. As a result of the action, three civilians were killed and three died of heart attack. There was significant light damage around the city. It was then that I lost faith in official Army communiques. The following is a summary of the facts as they took place.

The aircraft, which caused the alert, was a Navy anti-submarine search plane. Radio contact was finally established, and the plane was ordered back to base. It was never over or close to the city of Los Angeles. Coordination between the Army and Navy was only in the early stages of development.

The officer in charge of the operations center was relatively new and could not understand what a balloon was doing over Los Angeles. With the lessons of Pearl Harbor still fresh in his mind, he was taking no chances. To be on the safe side, he ordered a full air-raid alert for the Los Angeles area. He further ordered all searchlights to illuminate the balloon.

Early in the war, antiaircraft guns did not have radars. They had to visually see a target in order to engage it. At night, it relied on the searchlights to illuminate the target for them. Their standing orders for night engagement were that anytime the beams of three lights illuminated a target, they were free to fire at the intersection of the three searchlight beams.

According to the laws of physics, all that goes up, must come down. Therefore, thousands of pieces of shrapnel and unexploded rounds rained down upon the city. At that time, the large 3 inch antiaircraft shells used powder train fuses of World War I vintage. They were unreliable and 5-10 % returned to earth without having been exploded. This gave the effect of the city being hit with hundreds of small bombs. In addition to the personnel casualties, there were quite a number of buildings which also suffered damage.

The after effects of the attack were quite significant. The next day there was a large exodus from the city to safer interior areas. There were even attempts to move some defense industries away from the coastal areas.

Ernie Pyle, the famous war correspondent of World War II, was in Palm Springs at the time. He was staying at the Desert Inn, and he reported that the area was suddenly flooded with the rich and famous from Los Angeles. He reported that a number of them even brought their valuables with them and put them in storage there, so they would be safe for the duration of the war.

My experience with the after effects of the "air raid" was a little different. A short time later, I was invited to have Sunday dinner with a nice family that lived nearby. During the meal the father brought up the subject of the "air attack." I tried to explain that no Japanese air planes attacked Los Angeles. He became a little upset. He said that he knew better. He said that he was a World War I veteran and that he was the air raid warden for his area. He was out on duty that night and he had his binoculars with him. He said he counted 70 planes in the attack. Again I tried to explain that there were no enemy planes in the attack. It was to no avail. He told me that he knew that the Army ordered us to say that no planes attacked the city so as not to frighten the civilians, but he knew better.

After repeated efforts had failed, the "devil" made me take a different approach. I told him confidently that there were really 120 planes in the attack. He jumped up from his seat at the table and in a loud voice to his wife, said, "See, Martha, I told that it was a big Japanese air attack." If some how, or some where, you hear that there were 120 Japanese aircraft in the attack on Los Angeles, you now know the origin of that report.

The last time we went on full alert in Los Angles was during the Battle Of Midway. We were told that the Japanese fleet was at sea, but Headquarters didn't know exactly where. Intelligence indicated that there would be an air attack somewhere on the United States, within the next four or five days. The air attack took place at Dutch Harbor, Alaska.

At this point, I believe that it would be appropriate to add a few comments about the treatment we received from the people of the Los Angeles/Hollywood area. We were treated royally by everyone, including, "the high and mighty." In the 10 months that we were there, I never heard of a single instance where any member of our battery was the subject of anything of a disparaging nature.

All Hollywood was unbelievably supportive. Major stars, such as Bing Crosby, Bob Hope and Gary Cooper, went out of their way to be friendly and helpful to nearby units. I was given rides by Red Skelton and Pat OBrien to where ever I wanted to go, even if it was 15 - 20 miles out of their way. Their most common practice was to leave their recreation rooms with showers and cots open 24 hours a day for our use. Some would even have a refrigerator stocked with food and soft drinks.

William Goetz, the founder of Universal Studios would invite us to come, as we were, into his living room. There he showed us previews of his latest films.

The general population was equally supportive. We were always being invited to peoples' homes for dinner. It was not unusual when we were in a restaurant or tavern to have one of the customers pick up the tab. I remember going to the Hollywood Bowling Alleys, bowling a few games and having a couple of beers. Then, when I returned to our radar site and counted my change, I would have more money than when I started.

There was the Stage Door Canteen, and almost every community had a USO. Since we worked through the night, and were off during the day, USO personnel went out of their way to be of service to us. They would arrange picnics and beach parties for us with the girls who also worked at night (swing shift in the aircraft factories). They provided all of the food and beverages. All we had to do was to show up and enjoy ourselves.

This was in sharp contrast to the ugly treatment that was accorded to our service personnel in later years by Jane Fonda and her ilk.

The "Three Musketeers" from Saint Paul's:

Courtesy: Genero Family Collection

Peter - Charlie - Artie

67

Artie was by far the best soldier in the battery. He was promoted to be our First Sergeant.

Charlie was the most respected and best liked soldier in the battery. He was promoted to Platoon (Staff) Sergeant.

I became a Sergeant (T4) Chief radar operator and a searchlight/radar section chief.

The Army was expanding rapidly and there was a great need for additional officers. There was the general feeling among our group from Saint Paul's that it would be nice if one of us became an officer. One of the advantages of enlisting as a group was that we could help one another.

Since Artie was the best soldier in our battery, his was the first name submitted as a candidate for Officer Candidate School (OCS). When higher headquarters examined his file, they found that Artie did not have the math background to handle the three dimensional gunnery required for antiaircraft artillery officers.

Naturally, the next in line was Charlie. He was the logical choice since he had been to college, was an outstanding soldier, and had the necessary math background. His application was returned because he was too short. Minimum standard height was 5' feet 6 inches, and Charlie was only 5 feet 5 inches tall.

They finally got down to me. I was a fair soldier; I was 5 feet 9 inches tall; and thanks to De La Salle, I had the necessary math background. My application was submitted to higher headquarters. I was surprised that it was approved for further processing. The most important step of the processing was an appearance before the Officer's Review Board.

I seemed to have been doing reasonably well until they asked me where were the Caroline Islands. I immediately replied, "Off the coast of Carolina". Sensing that I had given the wrong answer, I told them that my answer was incorrect, and that I did not know where the Caroline Islands were. The Caroline Islands were Japanese fortified islands in the Central Pacific, which they used as a base for their attack on Pearl Harbor.

When I left, I was certain that I failed and consoled myself with feeling that, "At least I tried."

In October, 1942, our battery received two sets of traveling orders. One set ordered the immediate deployment of our searchlight battalion to North Africa. The second set of orders directed Sergeant (T4) Peter P. Genero to report to Officer Candidate School at Camp Davis, North Carolina.

CHAPTER - 7

OFFICER CANDIDATE SCHOOL (OCS)

Preface:

Going to Officer Candidate School(OCS) was a milestone in my life. See photo.

I was now in uncharted waters with no one to help me or guide me in my efforts. Prior to my military service, the family filled that role. While in the military service in the enlisted status, it was the "Gang of 10" from Saint Paul's, that was there whenever I needed them. This was the first time in my life that I was completely on my own.

In all honesty, I would not have been unhappy if my orders to OCS were cancelled, and I was ordered back to my outfit, which was on its way to North Africa.

Officer Candidate School
Tale of the Scrub Brush
After Graduation

Courtesy: Genero Family Collection

SERGEANT (T 4) PETER P. GENERO
ENROUTE TO OFFICER CANDIDATE SCHOOL

Officer Candidate School (OCS):

When I arrived at the Officer Candidate School (Antiaircraft Artillery) at Camp Davis, NC, I was pleasantly surprised. For the first time during my two years of military service, I was going to be billeted in a real wooden barrack with indoor plumbing.

Initially, there were about 75 candidates per building. They came from two main sources. About 20% were from the enlisted ranks. Mostly, they were former First Sergeants or other senior Non-Commissioned Officers. The remaining 80%, were from the Teachers Volunteer Program. This program was established to give direct commissions to qualified professors, teachers, and individuals with advanced degrees. They were given about 6 weeks of basic training and then sent directly to OCS. If they "washed out," they were returned back to civilian life.

About 70% of the course was classroom work, about 15% physical training. marching, drilling, etc., and 15% working with the weapons and firing them. As could be expected, the volunteers had little trouble with academics but had significant problems with learning how to be a good soldier, such as fixing beds, shining boots and brass, marching, customs of the service, and especially, how to give commands effectively. The former enlisted candidates had no trouble with being " a good soldier", but quite a bit of a problem with academics, especially gunnery. I was fortunate in that I was an "in between" candidate. My prior enlisted service helped me with being "a good soldier", and my De La Salle training helped me with the academic side of the training. My only drawback was my age. I was only 21 years old. I was one of the youngest candidates in our barrack.

**FOOT
LOCKER
READY FOR
INSPECTION**

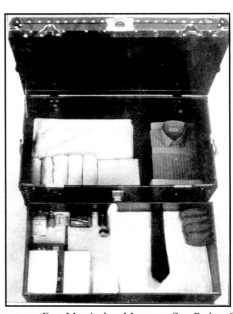

Courtesy: Fort MacArthur Museum, San Pedro, CA

Active training lasted about 10 hours each day, with a 2 hour study period at night. The only free periods were Saturday afternoons, if the inspection on Saturday morning was satisfactory. Sunday mornings were also free (church). Discipline was severe. Some units required that all movement outside of the barrack be "at attention" and in marching sequence, even when going to the Post Exchange.

The course lasted three months, hence the popular term, "ninety day wonder," when referring to newly commissioned Second Lieutenants. Attrition was quite high. Only about 35 of the original 75 candidates in our barrack successfully completed the course. The candidates were constantly being rated by the instructors, battery officers, and even by each other. Each Monday morning was elimination time, and each week there were a few additional empty cots in the barrack .

Probably the most surprising situation that I encountered took place on Monday night, the first week after my arrival. After our study hall, I walked back to my barrack. As I walked by the parade grounds, I kept hearing a multitude of voices, shouting out the entire repertoire of military commands. There were about 30-40 candidates scatterered over the parade grounds marching at attention, back and forth across the parade grounds, in the dark. Also, they were shouting military commands as loudly and as forcefully as they could. After observing them for a while, I finally realized what they were doing. They were almost all from the Teacher's Volunteer Program. They were practicing their marching and the giving of commands. One of the quickest ways of "washing out" of OCS was for a candidate not being able to march or give commands in a military manner. Practicing at that hour was because it was one of the few times of the day available to the candidate. Also, practicing in the dark helped preserve their anonymity.

The next semi-amusing situation took place during my first free Saturday evening. A group of us went to the nearby city of Wilmington. Trying to overcome the monotony of army chow, we asked for the best restaurant in town. We were told that it was in the Cape Fear Hotel. We went there and were seated at a comfortable table. I odered a "large" steak. It was not large by any standard, only about 1/2 inch thick and about 3 inches in diameter. I laughingly told my buddies that I was glad that I did not order a "small" steak. It was the last time that I went to Wilmington.

After that experience, I developed a simple and comfortable routine for Saturday afternoons. US Highway 17 (New York to Florida), was adjacent to Camp Davis. On it, near the rear entrance to our camp was a typical "country store." The type one sees in the movies. A couple of us would go there for a nice quiet and relaxing afternoon. I would buy a large fresh baked roll, a stick of salami, and a bottle of New York's premium brew (Ballantine Ale). How it ever found its way down to a country store in North Carolina, I do not know.

Tale of the Scrub Brush:

Every Saturday morning, each barrack was subjected to an intensive inspection.

The first Saturday, our barrack failed. We then had to prepare for a second inspection later that afternoon, and we were restricted to the Camp. The "old soldiers" taught the volunteers how to prepare better for inspection, even going to the extent of having them buy a complete second set of toilet articles: one for the inspection and one for daily use. However, the greatest problem areas we faced were the common areas: the stairwells, showers and latrine. The inspecting officers carried their inspection of these areas to the extreme. We all pitched in to make them acceptable.

74

We passed the afternoon inspection, but were still restricted to the Camp.

It so happened that on the second week, I was detailed to prepare the common areas for inspection. I worked almost the entire night cleaning these areas. The white pine wooden steps were scrubbed until they were almost white. Dirt and residue were cleaned out of all the cracks and corners. In the showers and latrines, the floors and walls were spotless. Probably of most importace, all the plumbing fixtures were not only cleaned, but shined to a sparkling brilliance. My skills were derived from a lifetime of experience working with my sisters and brother in both Rosendale and the city.

Saturday morning, the inspecting officers arrived and we all held our breaths. They did their usual exceedingly thorough job. The results were posted at noon. We not only passed the inspection, but had the unique and unusual experience of being awarded a commendation as well.

Next in the sequence of events was a little surprising. The folloing day, a number of the candidates held a meeting to discuss the Saturday morning inspections. The conclusion was that a delegation was formed and came to visit me. They asked if I would volunteer to prepare the common areas for inspection for the remainder of the course.

In a way, I guess, I felt honored and agreed. I performed the same task every Friday night for the remainder of the time until graduation. We did not always received a commendation, but we never failed another inspection.

My volunteering had a secondary effect. As mentioned previously, one of the evaluations the candidates received was the one given to him by his fellow candidates. Volunteering for this task insured that I would be placed near the top of the rating list submitted by all the other candidates. Barring the occurrence of any major unfavorable event, I was assured of graduating.

After graduation, my fellow officer candidates spoke of awarding me a "golden scrub brush." With the hustle and bustle accompanying graduation, they failed to find one. However, almost all of them stopped by and offered their personal thanks and appreciation.

After Graduation:

After graduation, we were all asked where we would preferred to go for our next assignment. Naturally, I volunteered for overseas duty, specifically, North Africa. I had envisioned joining my old buddies who were already there.

Typical of the Army, only half of my request was granted. I was granted an overseas assignment, but the area that I was assigned to was the South Pacific. As things turned out, this had the earmarks of a little help from above.

We were given a week's furlough to go home and visit our folks before being shipped overseas.

This was in February, and in Rosendale it was below zero. There was 2-3 feet of snow on the ground. Not desiring to spend the whole furlough being cooped up in the old homestead, I decided to take a walk to the village. There, I met Gerard Buckley, an old and close friend of the family. I was surprised to see that he was dressed exactly as I was. He too had just graduated from OCS (Infantry) and was on his final leave before being sent overseas. He was going to North Africa.

At the end of the war, I returned home. Gerard didn't.

CHAPTER 8

WORLD WAR II - SOUTH PACIFIC

Preface:

This may be the most disappointing and uninteresting chapter in the book. It covers my two and a half years in the South Pacific during World War II.

I did not participate in any of the real gory aspects of the Pacific conflict. I did not have to dig out any Japanese from any caves or jungle hide-outs, nor was I subjected to any of their fabled BANZAI attacks. In fact with only a few minor exceptions, the only Japanese that I saw were POW's in our prison camps.

Being in Antiaircraft Artillery, our job was to protect our air fields from Japanese air attacks. Even in this matter, we were quite fortunate. As the Japanese kept losing more and more airplanes, their air attacks against our airfields became fewer and fewer. Basically, we would protect an airfield until the air attacks ceased. Then, we would move forward to another airfield on another island. Since most of the enemy air attacks were at night, this left us free during the day to unload/load ships, stack tons of supplies in supply depots, help control malaria, and other base support activities.

Our biggest problem was in learning how to live and survive in a hostile jungle environment. There were all sorts of strange diseases, animals, and reptiles to contend with.

I wasn't stung by any venomous creature, although there were scorpions and snakes all over the place. One day a snake fell from our thatched roof and landed on the floor next to me. I grabbed a pole and beat it to death so severely and for so long, that I never was able to identify it.

From the disease viewpoint, there were many problems. Malaria was the worst and thankfully, I was spared from it. I did manage to pick up a mean local fever, but recovered after a few days in the dispensary. By far the most painful and difficult disease was what we called "jungle rot." It was extremely uncomfortable, and I did not get clear of it until I returned to the United States and a more temperate climate.

Again, I'm sorry to disappoint the reader with no exciting tales of war in the Pacific. On a few islands we were lucky and encamped in an old coconut plantation. This helped me answer questions concerning what I did during the war. My standard response was, "I counted coconuts." (Again, maybe with a little help from above.)

Attached is a sketch showing my travels in the Pacific.

Fiji islands
Espiritu Santo
New Caledonia
Guadalcanal
Green Island
Bougainville
Lae-Hollandia
Leyte

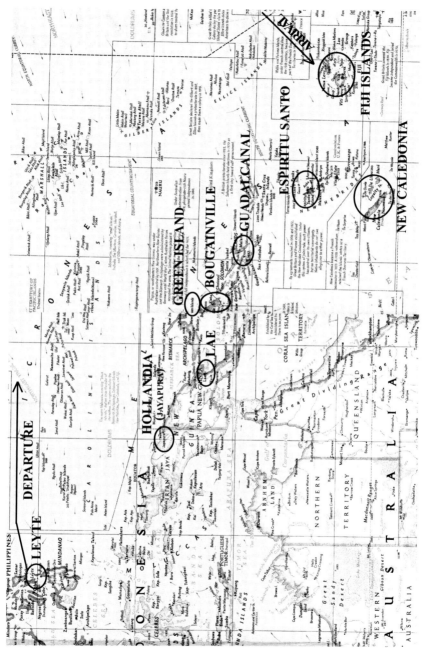

Courtesy: GABELLIUS, Miami, FL

SOUTH PACIFIC

Fiji Islands:

After graduation, about 60 brand new Second Lieutenants at Camp Davis received orders to Camp Stockton in California (near San Francisco). From there, we were to be shipped to the South Pacific.

On a cold rainy night in March, we were loaded aboard the Navy transport, Bloemfontein. It had been a former Dutch semi-luxury ocean liner that spent most of its time in the Dutch East Indies. It was about 10,000 tons and could carry about 2,500 soldiers/sailors.

After the Germans invaded Holland, the ship found its way into a United States port. There, it was chartered as a troop ship by the US Navy. It still retained its original Dutch crew.

We sailed without escort since they believed that the ship was fast enough to avoid enemy submarines. One of the features that contributed to its speed was its unique "speed boat bow," similar to those on small pleasure motor speed boats. We headed south and sailed across the Pacific Ocean in the Southern Hemisphere. It seemed that we traveled forever without seeing land. Actually, it was only about 26 days. I never realized that the Pacific Ocean was so large.

The Fiji Islands left me with two impressions, neither of which were favorable. The waters around the islands were beautiful, as on the post cards. However, the bay was sprinkled with hundreds upon hundreds of ugly giant jelly fish. They were about two feet in diameter and colored a sickening purple. Their tentacles were about 2-3 feet long and were very venomous. Needless to say, I did no swimming in the Fiji Islands.

The other situation concerned ginger beer. One day while walking down one of their dirt roads, I became very thirsty. I stopped at a roadside café. It also was right out of a Hollywood movie set. Across the doorway, hung long strings of brightly colored beads.

There was no door and to enter, one had only to spread the strings of beads apart and enter. Inside, there were 3 or 4 old unpainted wooden tables and a few chairs. Overhead hung a large electric ceiling fan, slowly turning in an effort to provide some comfort.

I sat at one of the tables and asked for a beer. I was told that the only beer that they had was warm "ginger beer." I told them that any kind of beer was OK. The waiter brought a bottle and poured it into a glass. Being thirsty, I hastily took three or four gulps of ginger beer. I gagged violently and almost threw up all over the place. I had never tasted ginger beer before and I could not believe the taste. It tasted exactly like hot soapy water. It took me two days to get that disgusting taste out of my mouth.

The only time that I had ginger beer afterwards was about 15 years later. Someone invented the Moscow Mule cocktail. The ginger beer had lots of ice and it was mixed with vodka and fresh lime juice.

Espiritu Santo:

Espiritu Santo is one of the largest islands of the New Hebrides group. They were jointly ruled (1906 - 1980) by the British and French with a condominium form of government. Since the Free French movement was strong there, both the British and French welcomed the arrival of US troops (100,000). This was to be the main Allied base to halt the Japanese expansion southward from the Solomon Islands. One of the tragic events of World War II occurred there a couple of months prior to our arrival.

The troop ship, President Coolidge (22,000 tons, 5,500 troops), was sunk in the bay by a mine. Aboard was one of the last true "horse cavalry" units of the US Army. It was thought that the horses and mules could be used effectively in the jungles of the South Pacific. All of the troopers made it to shore safely. The animals did not.

We stayed there only a few days, but it was sad to realize that all those animals were still lying in the holds of the ship, below us at the bottom of the bay. The thought remains with me till the present day.

It may be of interest to note that the US Navy assigned a Lieutenant Commander to these islands as a naval historian. Using these islands as a setting, he wrote a Pulitzer Prize winning book, which was turned into an extremely popular Broadway show and a hit Hollywood movie. The hero of the book was a French Planter who volunteered to become a "coast watcher."

Most "coast watchers" were New Zealanders or Australians. Their operations were extremely valuable to the Allied war effort in the South Pacific. They were former owners or managers of the many plantations (mostly coconut) on the islands. Normally, they were landed at night via submarine on Japanese held islands and lived with friendly natives. Equipped with radios, they reported on Japanese movements and activities. I can attest to their effectiveness, which will be explained later. The name of the Lieutenant Commander was James A. Michener and the title of his story was *South Pacific*.

New Caledonia:

In April 1942, we disembarked at Noumea, New Caledonia, the headquarters of all US forces in the South Pacific, Admiral Halsey, commanding. We were sent to an Army replacement depot for processing and shipment to our final destination.

The camp itself was merely a few acres of tents to provide shelter for the replacements. We had only routine housekeeping duties, while awaiting further orders. We were permitted to go to the City of Noumea and visit the French Officers Club.

Guadalcanal had sent an urgent request for 25 of us new antiaircraft Second Lieutenants. Since there would be no convoy for a couple of weeks, the Navy gave permission to have us flown there. It was sort of a haphazard arrangement. Each morning a few of us were to go to the nearby Naval landing strip and wait until there was some room on one of the cargo planes heading north to Guadalcanal.

A group of us decided that we would have our final night in town at the French Officers Club. Champagne was strictly rationed, only about 4 or 5 bottles a day. Normally they would start serving them at 5 o'clock and within thirty or forty minutes, it was all gone. Strange, but this night the champagne lasted until about 8 o'clock. When we returned to camp, we were well fortified by the champagne.

The next morning, I was the only one who managed to show up at the air strip. I climbed aboard an old Marine C-47 cargo plane. I stretched out on top of the cargo and rested till we got to Guadalcanal.

I don't know whether it was because our family had a bottle of wine on the table for every meal, or whether it was another instance of having a little help from above. However, the fact that I was the first officer replacement to arrive in Guadalcanal had a monumental impact on my future military service. This gave me seniority over the other 24 Second Lieutenants who were sent there. It meant that I was the first to be promoted to First Lieutenant and one of the very few to come home as a Captain.

Guadalcanal:

Our plane landed at Henderson Field without incident. However, when they opened the cargo doors of the old C-47, I was overwhelmed by the extreme heat, oppressive humidity, and odious smell of the jungle. It took a couple of hours before I was able to operate effectively.

The reason why there was such an urgent need for us replacement antiaircraft officers on Guadalcanal was a little unusual. The 214th Antiaircraft Regiment, Georgia (Milledgeville) National Guard, had relieved the 3d Marine Defense Battalion. The Marines had protected Henderson Field during the horrific days when the Japanese were attempting to re-take the field. They were quite worn out from the fighting, living conditions, and diseases. When relieved, they simply took their rifles and personal equipment, climbed aboard a troop ship, and sailed back to a rear area for rest and recuperation. They had left all of their antiaircraft guns and equipment on the island, in position, exactly where they had been using them.

The 214th seeing the opportunity to increase their firepower, organized a "provisional" battalion, and took over the Marine's guns and equipment. They levied the other units for the necessary enlisted personnel but were woefully short of officers. We were brought in to fill that gap.

When I arrived, because of my previous experience, I had expected to be assigned to the radar/searchlight battery. However, because of the above, I was assigned to a 90mm gun battery. This was fortunate since shortly thereafter, searchlights were phased out of operational use.

By the time I had arrived on Guadalcanal, the Japanese had settled into a routine for their air attacks. Since daylight air attacks were too costly, they limited their attacks to the nights. Because they lacked advanced navigation aids, they waited until the moon was at least half full. Unless there was severe weather, invariably we could expect an air attack every night during these periods. Needless to say, we became very familiar with the phases of the moon.

Official US Navy Photograph

NAVY HELPING ARMY - GUADALCANAL - 1943

The attached photo is an unrealistic staged photograph, but it evolved from a slightly amusing story.

About every week or so, the chaplain, i.e. morale officer, would arrive at our battery at sundown with a small 16mm movie projector. Because electric power was needed to operate our radar, we were one of the few military units in the area that had an electric generator to power the movie projector. We would tie a few bed sheets to a couple of coconut trees to serve as a screen for the films. I think I saw *Hopalong Cassidy Serves A Writ* six times. It was common practice for units to visit their neighbors and watch whatever films were being shown. One night while we were watching a film, there was an air attack. We shut off the film and ran to the guns and fired at the attacking planes.

The next day we were besieged by a large group of sailors and Navy photographers. It seems that the night before, there were a number of visiting sailors watching our film. When the alarm sounded, having no place to go, they jumped into the gun revetments with our men. When the firing started, the sergeants put them to work helping to pass the ammunition.

When their Navy commander heard this, he put his public relations staff into action. They wanted photographs of how their men helped the Army repel(?) an enemy air attack. They could not get all of the guns into one photograph, so they had all of the sailors standing around a single gun revetment.

The situation was so unreal that I declined to participate. However, I kept a copy of the photograph to show-off our gun revetments. They were probably the best ones the South Pacific. Since I had scrounged the materials and supervised their construction, I was quite proud of them.

About this time we were involved in another unusual incident. An Army fighter pilot received an air medal and a reprimand for the same engagement. The Army Air Corps was trying to help defend against night air attacks. They devised a new tactic in which one of their fighter planes would circle over the island above 20,000 feet. They would engage any enemy planes illuminated by search lights and flying above that altitude. We would engage any enemy plane below that altitude. One night when we opened fire at a bomber, we were surprised to see tracers from a fighter plane also engaging the same plane. It appeared that his tracers shot down the bomber.

When he landed, the pilot was asked why he violated the rules of engagement. He replied that the antiaircraft fire couldn't hit anything, so he decided to take over. He sort of changed his mind later when he examined his fighter plane. It was so badly damaged by antiaircraft fire that it was scrapped. Hence, he was given an air medal for shooting down a Japanese bomber, and a reprimand for violating the rules of engagement and losing his own plane.

The next interesting event took place on June 16th, 1943. It involved the "coast watchers." Through their efforts, a great victory was achieved and we did not incur serious losses. At this time the Allies were assembling a large invasion force to launch an attack on Japanese held New Georgia Island, and then, if successful, go on up the chain of the Solomon Islands to Rabaul. The Japanese decided to halt the attack by destroying the invasion fleet which was assembling off shore. It was to be a very large air attack with over 120 airplanes, one of the largest since the Battle of Midway.

The "coast watchers" near the Japanese airstrips watched the planes take off, counted them, saw them assemble, and head towards Guadalcanal. They were fighters, dive bombers, and torpedo planes. The coast watchers radioed this information to headquarters and as a result we had two hours warning of the impending attack. Immediately, every bomber and cargo plane that could fly evacuated the island. Every fighter plane was armed, fueled and took to the air to intercept the Japanese.

The engagement that ensued was one of the biggest Allied victories of the war up until that time. The estimates were that of the 120 planes, 77 were shot down, with a loss of only 7 of our fighter planes. The "coast watchers" counted the number of Japanese planes that returned, and confirmed that the number of 77 planes shot down was probably correct. The score for our battery was one Japanese plane and one Purple Heart.

Probably the most interesting part of the attack took place about a couple hours later. It seems that one of the few ships that were hit had a cargo, which included canned beer. As a number of cases floated ashore on our beach, the gun crews rushed into the water and rescued them. They had not tasted beer for months and needless to say, they enjoyed every last drop (despite the fact that the beer was warm).

It was about this time also that one night a PT boat commander got careless. His boat was struck and cut in half by a Japanese destroyer. Most of the crew made it safely to shore, but it was on a Japanese held island. Once again, it was the "coast watchers" who came to their rescue and arranged their return to safety. The torpedo boat was the PT 109 and the careless skipper was John F. Kennedy

The move up the chain of Solomon Islands was successful. After heavy fighting, the battle for the island of New Georgia was immortalized by the ballad, "Roger Young." He was awarded the Congressional Medal of Honor, posthumously.

A short time later, there was another interesting event, which perhaps should be mentioned. One day it seemed that there were about 100 military police (MPs) swarming all over the place. I didn't know that there were that many on the island. They were making sure that all latrines were properly screened, and that the soldiers swimming and washing their vehicles in the Lunga River were adequately covered.

The next day a naval warrant officer buddy gave us the answer. The previous day he was walking along the dirt road when a military sedan passed him. An elderly female with an unattractive face (his words) looked at him and waved to him. It was Eleanor Roosevelt. It did not boost our morale, but I guess that it gave a boost to her morale. This was to our advantage since it paid to have a friendly voice in Washington. We were at the bottom of the totem pole in so far as support from Washington was concerned. Washington's efforts were almost totally focused on Europe.

Often, natives were employed to help stack supplies in the supply depots. A truck would go to their village, load as many as they could onto the truck, and take them to the depots. The surprising thing was that as they were traveling down the dirt road, the natives would be joyfully singing "You Are My Sunshine" in perfect harmony.

Green Island:

Things finally settled down to routine, and we began preparing for our next move forward. It turned out to be a tiny atoll named Green Island. It was the closest island to Rabaul, the largest Japanese base in the South Pacific. Green Island was midway (about 20 miles) between Rabaul and Bougainville. Green Island was also the daytime hiding place for the Japanese re-supply barges running between the two islands. The task of taking the island was assigned to the Third New Zealand Infantry Division. They had no heavy antiaircraft guns of their own, so we were designated to fill that void.

As our convoy approached Green Island we were attacked by about 15 Japanese dive bombers. One of them was an old, open cockpit biplane, with a leather helmeted pilot, ancient goggles, et al. He flew on the deck about 50 -75 feet to the rear of our Landing Ship Infantry (LSI). I'll swear that he was looking directly at me when he passed. He tried to bomb our escorting destroyer, but all he managed was a near miss.

The photo shows our LST convoy under air attack, while it was approaching Green Island. Our radar and guns were on the lower deck.

Courtesy: US Naval Archives, Washington, DC

CONVOY UNDER ATTACK

At "H" Hour, New Zealand Commandos and Assault Infantry, landed at our beach and established a beachhead about 200 yards deep. At "H" +1, we disembarked from our landing ship and immediately began clearing a site in the jungle for our gun emplacements. About an hour later, I was surprised to see a number of New Zealand Infantrymen, who had apparently abandoned their perimeter defense positions and were walking by our site. I became worried and asked one of them what had happened. "Had the Japanese launched a counter attack?" He looked suprised and said, "No Sir. It's tea time." So went our first day of combat (?) on Green Island.

The campaign turned out to be a "cake walk." The island was not fortified, and there were only a couple hundred logistics type troops on the island. The New Zealanders took care of the situation in a couple of days.

During our stay on Green Island both Jack Benny and Bob Hope, and their troupes, stopped by for a few hours to entertain the troops. Hollywood again showing their support for the troops in the field. However, our battery was on the opposite side of the lagoon. We had to leave an officer and a skeleton crew on site, while the rest of the men went over to see the show. On both occasions, I was the designated officer who stayed behind.

It's ironic that Green Island was also the closest US air base to Truk, the main Japanese Naval base in the Pacific. Truk was in the middle of the Caroline Islands. Too bad I didn't know that when I had appeared before the OCS Selection Board.

An added item of interest. What happened to the natives? As shown below they were evacuated via LST to a nearby island to insure their safety.

Courtesy: US Naval Archives, Washington, DC

EVACUATION OF NATIVES FROM GREEN ISLAND

Bougainville:

Our next move was more in the nature of an administrative type move. It was to the Island of Bougainville. It was a large island about 130 miles long and about 30 miles wide. The mountain range down through the center of the island had peaks over 9,000 feet high. There we were to join the Americal Division (only division without a numerical designation) and the 37th Division for an assault on Luzon to recapture Manila.

On Bougainville the Americans had only a small beachhead (about 2 miles deep and 4-5 miles long) in the isolated area of Empress of Augusta Bay. The Japanese were on the other side of the mountains. Two airfields were built within our perimeter. The Japanese launched a major counter attack in an effort to eliminate the beachhead. They failed after suffering heavy casualties. The Americans counterattacked and tried to expand their beachhead. They too suffered significant casualties and withdrew back to their original beachhead.

There were constant patrols by both sides, but it almost seemed that an unofficial "gentlemen's agreement" had been reached. The Japanese kept to their side of the island, and we kept mostly to our perimeter. Occasionally, there were mortar shells and artillery shells lobed into the perimeter, but they were of no consequence. There were even reports of Japanese soldiers sneaking inside our perimeter at night to watch some of our movies.

Since we cut the Japanese supply lines, there was an attempt to try and starve them out. Strange, but we conducted daily airplane attacks with napalm on their vegetable gardens. It had only limited success. The jungle was loaded with edible products, and the ocean was teaming with fish.

Courtesy: Genero Family Collection

BATTERY A, 967 AAA GUN BATTALION BOUGAINVILLE - 1944

Author - First Row Seated - 8th from the end (either left or right)

93

This was a very busy time. There were no docks or piers. All cargos and equipment had to be moved across the beaches, loaded on to small landing crafts, and ferried out to the ships anchored off shore. However, through some miscalculation, they were one ship short. It was our ship, and we were left ashore.

The Americans were relieved by the Australians. They came in with about three divisions. Bougainville was an Australian mandated island. They were disappointed that we did not retake the whole island. The Australians indicated that they were going to correct that situation. They began to expand the beachhead. In the meantime, their cemetery also began to expand. Finally, the Australian generals decided that it would be a wise course of action if they too waited till the end of the war. The records are fairly conflicting, but it appears that when the Americans first landed, there were about 42,000 Japanese troops on Bougainville. At the end of the war, over 20,000 surrendered.

For a short while, we were the only Americans on the island with the Australians. It was not too bad because most of the rations in the food depots were from the United States, and we claimed that we should have first choice. The biggest problem that we had was trying to learn how to drive on the left side of the road.

Finally, someone in higher headquarters realized that we were left on Bougainville. They sent a ship for us, but for some unknown reason we ended up on Leyte instead of Luzon. It appears that once again I had a little help from above. The fighting on Luzon was intense and lasted till the end of the war. The fighting on Leyte had been fairly well contained.

Lae - Hollandia:

Our trip to Lae in new Guinea was uneventful. We picked up some more troops and waited for a suitable naval escort to Hollandia (Jayapura).

The taking of Hollandia was the epitome of MacArthur's brilliant "leapfrogging campaign." It avoided the Japanese strong points and enabled the Allies to advance more quickly to the Philippines. He left about 1,000,000 Japanese troops to whither on the vine in New Guinea, the Bismark Archipelago, and other islands of the South Pacific.

The bay at Hollandia was very large and could accommodate over 100 ships. It was the main staging point for further advancements, especially to the Philippines. When we had about 60-70 ships assembled, we sailed to the Philippines under heavy naval escort. I never did learn why they sent us to Leyte instead of Luzon.

The three weeks we spent aboard ship could almost be called a period of rest and recuperation. Duties were light. I slept in a bunk bed with clean white sheets. The food was excellent. There was fresh meat every day and even real potatoes. Best of all, we had ice cream several times a week. Even the cool distilled drinking water was a treat.

There was one personal factor which caused me to appreciate the boat trip more fully. I had mentioned previously that I had developed a bad case of "jungle rot" while on the islands. During my time on the ship, the infection was reduced considerably.

Leyte:

Initially, we were deployed around Leyte's capital city, Tacloban. Shortly thereafter, we were redeployed to defend the major US air base about 25 miles south, Dulag. We stayed there till the end of the war. There, our battery was located at the prolongation of the axis of the strip, in layman's terms, at the end of the runway. This location gave rise to an occurrence of a serious nature.

One morning, a fully loaded cargo plane tried to take off from the airstrip and didn't quite make it. It landed in cartwheel fashion right next to our battery. A group of us rushed to the smoking wreckage and pulled out the crew. They were still alive, but in very poor condition. I was a little embarrassed later to learn that I had been awarded the Soldier's Medal for my efforts.

During this period, the Infantry was trying to clean out a few pockets of Japanese soldiers still holding out in the nearby hills. On occasion, they would come out of their caves, conduct a small harassing operation, and then quickly return to the safety of their caves. Our standard artillery pieces (105mm howitzers) tried for weeks to close the caves but didn't succeed. Someone heard that our 90mm guns were very accurate and they asked for our help.

We took a couple of our guns, attached them to big bulldozers, and dragged them up into the mountains. One of our Lieutenants, John Smith from Punxsutawney, Pennsylvania, was put in charge of the operation. The guns were dragged up to an adjacent mountain from which our gunners could visually locate the Japanese caves. Once the caves were located, they had little trouble placing their rounds directly into the mouths of the caves. Using a delayed action fuses, the cave would be closed permanently. This forced the Japanese to be constantly digging new caves in which to hide. Their harassing activities were noticeably reduced. At the end of the war, about 2,000 Japanese soldiers, in clean uniforms, officers wearing white gloves, surrendered to our forces on Leyte.

With the exception of an occasional enemy reconnaissance plane, things around Dulag were quite peaceful. We were spending a lot of our time helping our companion units which were getting ready for Operation Olympic, the invasion of Kyushu, Southern Japan. Our battalion was being held in reserve for Operation Coronet, the follow-on main attack on the Tokyo-Yokohama area in central Japan.

All of this changed when the atom bombs were dropped on Hiroshima and Nagasaki. Japan agreed to unconditional surrender if they could keep their Emperor. There was considerable discussion in Washington and much time was spent negotiating with our Allies as to what our response should be. It was strange, but General MacArthur was the only Allied leader to publicly announce that we should accept the Japanese offer. On August 15, 1945, the Allies accepted the Japanese offer. THE WAR WAS OVER.

My immediate reaction was to remove all of the firing pins from our guns and the back plates from our machine guns. I locked them in the battery safe. I then went to visit my buddies and celebrate the end of the war. This left the men in the battery to have their own celebration, without the oversight of their battery commander. This is mentioned because sadly, it was not the action taken by other American troops.

On Okinawa, the troops celebrated by firing their cannons and machine guns into the air. They forgot that what ever goes up, must come down. The night sky was filled with tracers, streaming through the air. This gave the appearance of hundreds of roman candles (as used in 4th of July celebrations), being fired into the air above the troops. The carnage became so great, that the island commander had to declare an "air attack alert" to bring things back into control. That night, 28 servicemen died needlessly.

The next day we celebrated the end of the war with a giant Mass on the Dulag air strip. Thousands attended. The altar was mounted an a large flatbed trailer. It was shielded from the sun with a large white parachute. It was interesting to note that we declared war on December 8th (Feast of the Immaculate Conception of the Blessed Virgin Mary) and the war ended on August 15th (Feast of the Assumption of the Blessed Virgin Mary). The Immaculate Conception is the Patroness of the United States.

The remainder of this chapter falls into the "What If" category. "What If there was no atom bomb", or "What If", we decided not to accept the Japanese offer and we proceeded with the planned invasion of Kyushu. The scenario would not have been pleasant.

The invasion was scheduled for early October. On the 9th of October a severe typhoon (Louise) was several hundred miles south of Okinawa and headed due west to China. Suddenly, without warning, the typhoon with 35 foot waves, changed its course to due north, right at Okinawa and Kyushu. When it hit Okinawa, the damage was severe. Over 120 ships were sunk or severely damaged. Over 60 aircraft were severely damaged. About three fourths of all US military supplies on the island were severely damaged. One naval cruiser of 10,000 tons was beached on land, 125 yards from the shoreline. Thirty-seven servicemen were killed and hundreds injured. A few months earlier, Admiral Halsey's fleet was caught at sea in a similar storm. Three of his destroyers were lost with their entire crews.

All of this happened while the round bottomed, shallow draft landing ships, crafts, barges, etc. were in a protected harbor. Had this happened while the invasion fleet was at sea, or in the process of landing as was scheduled, it would have been the greatest military disaster in our nation's history.

Once again, Japan would have been saved by Kamikaze, the Divine Wind. It would have been similar to the Kamikaze storm, which destroyed the Mongolian invasion fleet in 1281.

CHAPTER 9

POSTWAR - US ARMY

Preface:

This was an interesting period of my life. I knew "what" I was doing, but did not know "where" I was going. It can be divided into three distinct periods.

The first period could be described as "happy times." We were all returning home. It was time for celebration and for looking forward to a life better than the pre-war depression and the austere war years.

The next was a transitional phase, during which the US Army was changed from the greatest army in the world into a mere paper tiger. It was caused by the unprecedented rapid demobilization of the armed forces, without regard to the consequences. There was one little incident which perhaps best describes the situation. A senior Army General in Europe was asked what the Soviet Union Army would need in order to defeat the American Forces and march across Europe to the Atlantic Ocean. The General's response was one word, "Boots."

The final section concerns the re-awakening of the nation to its world wide responsibilities. It began with the Blockade of Berlin.

Euphoria
Disintegration
Recovery

Euphoria:

The first six-eight months after the war was the real "happy time," both for myself and the entire nation. It started immediately after Japan agreed to accept the modified terms of "Unconditional Surrender."

After having spent two and a half years in the Far East, I was anxious to see what Japan really looked like. I volunteered to go to Japan and serve in the Army of Occupation, This was despite the fact that I had accumulated enough points to ensure that I would be one of the first troops rotated back to the states. It seems that while my request was being processed, I was ordered to return to the United States. Another instance of a little guidance from above?

Things continued in a positive manner. Initially, I was placed in command of troops (about 650) bunked in hatch number five of our returning troopship. It just so happened that all of the troops in hatch five were in the Army Air Corps. The troop ship commander decided (with a little help from the author), that since the troops were from the Air Corps, they should be commanded by an Air Corps officer. I was relieved of all duties and responsibilities. My trip back to the States was quiet, peaceful, and restful.

We landed at Tacoma, Washington, and moved to Fort Lewis for further processing. However, this was not before first encountering the harsh realities of life in the States. Shortly after docking, the Red Cross came aboard and gave us all the fresh baked doughnuts and all of the fresh milk we desired. Since we had not tasted real fresh milk in a couple of years, our internal organs were not quite equipped to handle the situation. However, within a day we had recovered from our distress and were overjoyed to be on our way home.

The happy times continued. The food served at the Fort Lewis Officer's Club was excellent and so was the service. Almost the entire kitchen/dining room staff was composed of German POW's. The railroad trip across country in standard Pullman cars was comfortable. We were pleased to once more see banks of clean white snow.

We arrived at Fort Dix, NJ, for our final processing before leaving the service. At our initial briefing, we were told that it would take an additional three days before we would be released to return home. We had to have a final physical examination, and our new 'rights" under the GI Bill had to be explained. We were to be given new uniforms and insignias, receive our "mustering out" bonus, etc. After being away from home for almost 5 years, except for a couple of short furloughs, I was unhappy at being so close but having to sit around for three more days.

I let them know of my displeasure. They responded by giving me an option that I could not refuse. I could be out of Fort Dix and on my way home in "three hours," if I would sign-over and agree to stay on active duty. This included a 45 day period of "rest and recuperation," not chargeable as "official leave." By coincidence, this included Thanksgiving, Christmas, and New Years. I asked, "Where do I sign?" Within three hours I was on my way home.

It was another instance in which I may have a little help from above. Had I been discharged at that time, I probably would have returned to my old job with the New York Central Railroad and have spent the rest of my life collecting ferry tickets.

I was home in our apartment in Woodside, Long Island, that same evening. I received a joyous family reunion. They were a little surprised that I had lost so much weight. I was down to 150-160 pounds. Of course this was corrected very shortly. However, I was surprised at my family's constant questions about my "malaria." I tried to explain that I did not have malaria.

It appears that they equated the yellow tint of my skin with malaria. For the first time, I realized that there was a pronounced yellow tint to my skin. It showed up vividly around my eyes and in the corners of my other facial areas. Since this pigmentation had taken place over the period of a couple years, I was unaware of the discoloration. It was caused by the daily dose of atabrine that we were required to take in the tropics. It was a very effective malaria suppressant. My skin gradually returned to its normal color when I stopped taking atabrine.

After my happy home coming, I began making daily afternoon and evening visits to our old neighborhood around Saint Paul's in Manhattan. It was one continuous round of parties and celebrations. It seemed that every day, another member of the old gang was returning home. These home comings were excuses for another party, celebration, and the telling of exaggerated "war stories." These were truly "happy times." With their "mustering out pay," there was very little serious "job hunting" by my buddies, which left more time for celebrations. Truthfully, I can not remember ever having such a fun filled 45 days before or since.

This continued even during the annual family ritual, which took place in Rosendale right after the first significant snow fall. It was hog butchering time. This was made tolerable with the liberal consumption of ginger ale, mixed with some of the latest batch of our family produced "rye." Of course, the weekend dances at the Rosendale Grange and local taverns also helped.

This post war "happy time" continued through Thanksgiving, Christmas and New Years. There wero so many parties and celebrations that it gave the appearance of being one 45 day long festival. Strange, but there are only two incidents which took place during this period that I remember vividly.

The first concerns our family's Christmas in Rosendale. Immediately after our Christmas celebration, the family excluding,

Mamma and Big Joe, started back to the city in my brother's car. In order to demonstrate my driving skills (having been a prime mover driver in the Army), I insisted on driving. About half way home, in New Jersey, it started to snow mixed with a little sleet.

I kept on driving, reciting a take-off of the motto of the Post Office. "Neither rain, nor snow, nor sleet, nor dark of night… will deter our carriers, …etc". Having never driven in snow or sleet before, I quickly slid off the road and into a ditch. No one was hurt. My brother, expert driver and mechanic, took control of the situation. He put chains on the tires, got us out of the ditch and back to the city safely. It was the last time that I ever bragged about my driving in front of the family.

The other incident took place in the ballroom of the Pennsylvania Hotel in the city. A group of us were attending a diner/dance there. During a dance break I strolled out into the foyer. Standing next to me was an extremely beautiful blond in a white evening gown. She was quite young, about 17 - 18, and appeared to be a little timid and out of place. When the music started again, I went back into the ballroom. The young blond was the vocalist for the band. The band was Les Brown and his Band of Renown. She sang, "I'm going to take a sentimental journey" (extremely popular among the home coming service men). The young girl's name was Doris Day.

All of this came to an end after New Years. I packed my bags, went to Penn Station, and headed for my next assignment at Fort Bliss, Texas. I was a little sad about leaving the city and going back to the Army. The train ride in the Pullman car was comfortable. It went as far as Saint Louis. There, we had to change trains for Texas. In those days there were no coast to coast through trains. Changing trains at Saint Louis or Chicago was the norm.

While waiting for my change of trains, I went to the cocktail lounge and ordered a scotch and soda. The bartender would not serve me unless I told him whether I want "sweet" soda or "dry" soda. Having never heard of "sweet" soda before, I got into a discussion with the bartender. A fellow customer came to my rescue. He explained that "sweet" soda and scotch was popular in Saint Louis (probably the only place in the world), and that what I wanted was a dry soda. This incident was symbolic of the change that was taking place in my life. The "happy times" of the past were ending, and the "trying times" of the future were just beginning.

When I boarded the Texas & Pacific Train in Saint Louis to go to El Paso (Fort Bliss), my feelings were reinforced that the good times were coming to an end. The passenger railroad car was evidently manufactured during the war and was intended for war time use only. It resembled a box car more than a standard Pullman car. The trip lasted three days, and it was the most uncomfortable railroad ride that I had ever taken. It was so bad that I made a vow to never again take an overnight trip on a railroad . It is now 62+ years later, and I have not broken that vow.

The officer accommodations at Fort Bliss were of a similar nature. I was assigned an 8'X10' tar paper shack,with no plumbing, in the middle of a desert. My duties were to give new recruits their basic training. The overall atmosphere appeared to be "listless," with an almost complete lack of motivation. I quickly applied for overseas duty with the Army of Occupation in Germany. Once again, I wound up in the Pacific.

It was during this period that I began to notice a change in public attitude towards the military, especially the officers. Perhaps, it was fueled by the popular publications of the day, such as *Time* and *Life* magazines. In an inordinate number of war stories, the heroes came from the enlisted ranks, while officers were generally portrayed as incompetent. The enlisted ranks deserved all of the praise that they could get. It was their blood, sweat and tears that won the war. However, there must also have been some competent officers in the field. Many officers found it expedient to wear civilian clothes when off duty.

My personal contact with this attitude came from an old buddy. We grew up together and had known each other for 15 years. He told me quite bluntly that he hated all officers and that he wanted nothing further to do with me. His wish was granted.

The overall situation was not at all similar to the outright vitriolic hostility shown to the service personnel during Vietnam. It was more of a subtle nature, such as the stories found in the popular media of the day. Perhaps, it can best be demonstrated by examining two of the most popular movies of that era; *The Best Years Of Our Lives* (winner of 7 Academy Awards), and later, *From Here To Eternity* (winner of 8 Academy Awards).

Despite the underling negative public perception of the officers at that time, I personally experienced one of the happiest days of my life. I married the very attractive and vivacious Betty Myers. A couple of months later she was able to join me in Japan.

The wedding was the last major happening of the Euphoric period.

Disintegration:

In Yokohama, I was astounded at the total destruction of the city. Not a building was left standing, except the few built of concrete and reinforced steel. The camp of Eighth Army Headquarters was in the center of the ruined city. The Army Engineers used bulldozers to simply level off about 10 square blocks of rubble and build their tent city on top of it. The total destruction was caused by the fire bombings of the city in March and May, 1945. The conditions during the raids were just right, dry weather and a strong wind. It created a fire storm of unbelievable proportions, extending all the way to Tokyo. Conservative estimates were that 100,000 people died. Fortunately, the area was crisscrossed with a network of barge canals. The people jumped into the canals. The older ones sat upon the shoulders of the younger ones. Had it not been for the canals, the total fatalities would probably have been greater than Hiroshima and Nagasaki combined.

When I arrived in Japan in the summer of 1946, I witnessed the full extent of the disintegration of the US Army. I was assigned to an Antiaircraft Artillery Group consisting of three battalions: a 120mm gun battalion; a 40mm automatic weapons battalion; and a self propelled (armored) .50 caliber machine gun battalion. We were responsible for the security of the metropolitan area of Yokohama, second only in importance to Tokyo. Besides being the headquarters for the US Eighth Army, it was the most important seaport in Japan. To accomplish this, we had about 125 security guard posts in and around the city and port facilities. These were manned by our troops 24 hours a day, seven days a week.

Our battalion had four 120 mm gun batteries. The personnel in these batteries worked in shifts as security guards, 6 hours on and 18 hours off. Each battery manned an entire shift, leaving behind only a couple of cooks to make coffee and prepare meals. Each weekend one of the shifts would be advanced so that the same battery would not be manning the same shifts, at the same times, on a continuous basis. There was no time left over for training on the guns, radars, or computers. The antiaircraft operational capability of the battalion was "zero."

Our equipment was parked in an old Japanese naval seaplane hangar, which was still useable. The equipment was being maintained by one old time gun mechanic and one radar repairman. They were given about 20 Japanese laborers to assist them. Combined, they were the only ones who knew how to turn on and operate the equipment. Also, they were the only ones who could place the guns in a traveling mode or a firing position. We were not capable of operating our own equipment. It was simply guard duty, guard duty, guard duty, every day, every week, every month. This situation remained in place without change until the summer of 1948.

The root cause of the problem was the unprecedented depth and rapidity of the demobilization of the Army at the end of the war. The officers were not immune from the effects of the demobilization. Because of the extreme and rapid downsizing of the Army, there were now too many officers for the number of troops still on duty. The Army instituted a random selection procedure for the immediate discharge of officers from active duty. When an officer awoke in the morning, he did not know if his name would be on the list for discharge that day. It gave the appearance of a giant lottery, with the winner being told to pack his bags and go home.

The status of the enlisted personnel was much more chaotic. The draft boards stopped drafting the most qualified individuals and began scraping the bottom of the barrel. They started selecting those who were deferred earlier because they were deemed not qualified for the military service. Those selected were given only rudimentary basic training and then sent to units in the field as replacements.

The following is such an example. I once received 12 new replacements. Within 30 days, I had the entire 12 administratively discharged from the service for being unable to perform their assigned duties. None of them could read, write, speak, or understand the English language.

The IQ's of the replacements barely met military standards. On another occasion, I received 22 new replacements. One of them had one year of high school education. He was immediately appointed to be the battery clerk. The remaining 21 replacements had no high school education whatsoever.

There was even the sad situation of an unfriendly judge in Philadelphia. He gave young criminals the choice of either going to prison or serving in the Army. A few performed their military duties in a satisfactory manner. The others continued with their criminal activities and spent their time in a military prison, as opposed to a civilian prison.

The officers were spending an inordinate amount of time preparing for, or participating in courts martials. Normally, it was not unusual for a battalion to have one or two of its members in the stockade. However, the average prison population of our battalion at this time was 35 to 40.

The ultimate chaotic situation occurred in another battalion. Things became so out of control that all small arms and ammunition were confiscated. They were locked in one of our old Japanese underground bunkers. The only weapon permitted in the entire battalion area was a pistol worn at the side of the Officer of the Day.

The entire Army of Occupation was in similar straits. Some units were less than 50% authorized strength. Infantry companies were down to two platoons, instead of three. Battalions were down to two companies instead of three, etc. We were a little more fortunate. Because of the importance of our mission, we were maintained near our authorized strength, mostly at the expense of the combat divisions.

There was one incident that took place in 1947, which clearly demonstrates the lack of discipline and control. It may appear to be amusing to some, but it could have erupted into a serious and deadly situation. It was the attack on Tokyo by a sea monster.

The incident involved the Armed Forces Radio Network in Japan. This was before television, and the only source for news, entertainment, and rapid dissemination of military orders was the Armed Forces Radio Network.

The radio network was routinely used for official announcements. As an example, its use was absolutely essential during sudden, secret currency exchanges. Troops did not receive US dollars, but were paid with military payment certificates, see below. Japanese were forbidden to possess such a certificate. This was an effort to curb the black market activities involving US personnel. Periodically, on a super secret date, over the radio, all US personnel would be ordered to report to their base immediately. There, they would exchange their old military payment certificates for new ones. At the end of the day, the old certificates would be worthless, and those involved in the black market would be left holding paper of no value.

Courtesy: Genero Family Collection

MILITARY PAYMENT CERTIFICATE - JAPAN 1948

The attack of the sea monster referred to, took place in April, 1947. Throughout the day, radio programs were being interrupted with reports of unusual disturbances off the coast of Japan. The listeners were asked to help and to report to the station any disturbance, which they witnessed. That evening, there were "flash" reports of a disturbance that had been sighted in Tokyo Bay. All troops in the Tokyo/Yokohama area were to be on the alert and report any strange sightings or disturbances.

Later the radio reported that a giant sea monster had come out of the bay and was destroying buildings and killing people in Tokyo. It reported that the military police were helpless because their bullets had no effect on the monster.

A professor from Tokyo University had identified the monster as having been living in the unexplored depths of the Pacific Ocean. The nearby Mindanao Trench is the deepest in the world. The professor hypostatized that it was driven from the depths as a result of the US atom bomb testing in the Pacific Ocean.

The radio broadcasts warned all military personnel to stay clear of the bay. Our house was on the bay, so I took my rifle and escorted my wife to a friend's house back from the shore. She insisted on taking the dog with us, as she did not want the monster to eat him.

The radio kept reporting on the destruction being wrought by the monster. Finally, it reported that an Army's chemical mortar battalion had been called in and was able to subdue the monster.

The radio announced that one of its reporters was near enough to the monster to hear its dying gasps. Then over the radio came a popular song of the day, "I'm a Reluctant Dragon." Then came the announcement, "Happy Birthday - Armed Forces Radio". (It was all a hoax)

Needless to say, all members of the radio staff who had any connection with the hoax, were fired the next day.

Miraculously there were no fatalities as a result of the incident. American harbor patrol craft with searchlights and machine guns had been immediately put out on patrol. Since our battalion was on the bay, all of our tracked armored vehicles were deployed along the coast. They were armed with .50 caliber machine guns. Their headlights were turned on and pointed out over the bay. The guns were loaded and the crews were free to engage any thing that looked like a monster. Had a Japanese fishing boat or any craft, even an allied patrol vessel been mistaken for a monster, it would have been blasted out of the water.

Similar protective measures were taken by other military units in the Tokyo - Yokohama area. Only these were mentioned because of my personal knowledge of them.

Years later, we were able to see the amusing side of the incident. Some even believe that the incident gave birth to the rash of Godzilla movies produced by the Japanese in later years. However, it clearly demonstrates the depths to which military discipline had sunk during this period. Also, it should be remembered that some of the fingers on the triggers of those machine guns did not belong to "The Best and the Brightest."

It was in March, 1948, that one of the biggest events of the Genero family took place. Our twin daughters, Laura-Anne and Linda-Anne were born in Yokohama. It was strange but one of the first thoughts that entered my mind was, would they be considered "natural born citizens," under the terms of Article II, Section 1, of the US Constitution?

Recovery:

The deteriorated state of the Army continued until the summer of 1948. There was an international incident, which caused a reversal of the whole situation. It was the Berlin Blockade, see Chapter 14. Fortunately, the nation had a president, Harry Truman, who was not afraid to make tough decisions. He not only handled the blockade successfully, but he reversed the entire downward trend in the readiness of the armed services.

Even the draft boards got the message. They began inducting better qualified personnel. By 1949, they were once again drafting high school graduates. It took a few months, but the improvements in the combat readiness of the armed services were quite noticeable.

Despite the above, the occupation of Japan will be recorded as one of the most successful military occupations in history. It was all the result of the masterful way in which it was handled by General Douglas MacArthur. Volumes and volumes have been written on the subject, so I will limit my comments to a few incidents of which I have personal knowledge.

The Japanese people respect authority. General MacArthur fitted that image perfectly. Whenever he entered or left his headquarters building, there would be crowds of normal Japanese citizens there to cheer him and pay him homage. He carried himself as was expected of a leader in an oriental country. There was no grinning, waving, shaking hands, as is customary with US politicians.

He set broad goals and sat back and let the Japanese implement them in their own fashion. He did not try to micro-manage the country. Only true war criminals were tried and punished. He left almost the entire industrial class in place. The Saibatsu (a loose society of industrial leaders, i.e., Mitsubishi, Nisan, etc.) was invaluable in the rebuilding of the economy of Japan.

There was land reform, and the formation of labor unions was encouraged. Later, the unions became a problem, but they were kept within bounds as the following situation will demonstrate.

At the end of war, the Soviets occupied Manchuria and North Korea. As a result, they captured about 350,000 Japanese soldiers and held them prisoner. The prisoners were subjected to intense "brain washing." The only ones permitted to return home were those who were converted to Communism. These were sneaked back into Japan individually or in small groups, through the hundreds of small ports and fishing villages along the Japanese coast. Their mission was to create labor unrest with the ultimate aim of taking control of the government.

Their attempt culminated in a massive demonstration (about 500,000) in Tokyo, organized by the government workers union. Our troops were alerted, and we formed strong points along the route of march. The troops were armed and their machine guns were fully loaded. Their orders were to open fire at the demonstrators if they were attacked, or if the demonstrators went on a destructive rampage. They were also authorized to open fire if the demonstrators tried to physically take over the government.

The demonstrators assembled and began their march. They waved banners, shouted slogans, and even sang the "Internationale", the Communist theme song. When they came to one of our strong points and saw the weapons pointed at them, they became quiet and meekly passed by. Once they passed by, they resumed their shouting, singing, and flag waving until they reached the next strong point. The process was continued until they arrived at the government sectors of Tokyo. After a few speeches, they quietly dispersed and went home. Our troops said that for a major demonstration, it was one of the most peaceful that they had ever seen.

At this point it should be mentioned that The Allied Council for Japan was in charge of the occupation of Japan. It was composed of representatives from all of the nations that had been at war with Japan. General MacArthur's primary duty was to implement the orders issued by the council. Soviet membership was a stumbling block. They pushed their own agenda, i.e., the Communization of Japan. Also, they blocked all actions with which they did not agree.

General MacArthur sent a memorandum to the Council requesting permission to have the Japanese establish a Coast Guard. He specifically wanted to stop the infiltration of brainwashed ex-Japanese soldiers who were creating problems. The Soviets filibustered the request. They claimed that we were trying to re-arm Japan.

General MacArthur waited about two weeks and then sent the Council another memorandum. He informed them that the need for a Coast Guard was so acute that he could wait no longer. As of that date, he had established a Japanese Coast Guard. As a sop to the Soviets, they named it the Japanese Maritime Safety Agency. (A short time later, it was officially called the Japanese Coast Guard).

There was one initiative that was begun with US aid and was so successful that its effects are still with us today. I personally witnessed its beginning. Since it was so extraordinary, I will spend a few paragraphs to describe what I witnessed. It was the birth of the Japanese mass production of automotive vehicles.

At the beginning of the occupation, there were only about 75,000 motor vehicles in all of Japan. The vehicles ranged from charcoal burning taxis to an unbelievable assortment of small and medium trucks. The nation relied almost entirely on its excellent rail system and its extensive network of barge canals. Short hauls were done by bicycle and oxcart.

To rejuvenate their industrial sector, Japan needed a large number of motor vehicles as soon as possible. The only readily available source was the thousands of motor vehicles abandoned by the US military on the hundreds of islands in the Pacific. It was less expensive to abandon them than to return them back to the US. The Japanese were authorized to retrieve these vehicles and bring them to Japan to be refurbished. We even lent the Japanese a number of surplus World War II Liberty Ships for that purpose.

Our battalion was stationed at a large Japanese naval seaplane base. The barracks and hangars escaped damage. On the base were two very large airplane hangars. We used one for our equipment. The other hangar was vacant. It was in front of this hangar that the Japanese dumped the remains of thousands of the retrieved motor vehicles.

About the same time, several teams of US automobile production engineers and assembly line supervisors were brought into Japan. One team was stationed with our battalion. A large number of Japanese workers was assembled. Under the supervision of the US team of experts, they established a refurbishing production line, as shown in the sketch.

Each junk vehicle was carried to the beginning of the assembly line. As it moved along the conveyor system, it was disassembled in a specific sequence. The parts were given to the cleaning crews in the middle of the hangar, where they were cleaned and repaired to meet original specifications. The parts were then moved to storage bins across the aisle, near the returning leg of the assembly line. The process was continued until the only remaining part of the vehicle was the engine block.

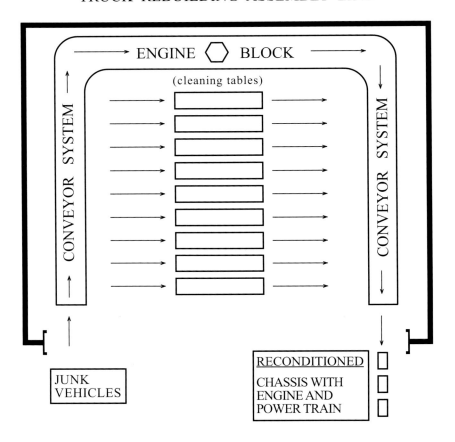

On the cross-over conveyor, the engine block was cleaned, re-bored, and rebuilt with whatever was needed. It was then moved to the return conveyor system. The engine, transmission, differentials, etc. were reassembled in the exact reverse order in which they were disassembled. At the end of the line, there was a complete operational truck chassis with engine and drive train. It was ready to be fitted with whatever type of truck body was desired.

It was astonishing to have witnessed the birth of an industry, which today surpasses its counterparts here in the United States.

One final incident occurred before we returned to the United States. Not long after the Berlin Airlift started, it was decided to begin serious training with our antiaircraft guns, and spend less time with our security guard duties. The Japanese were more and more taking over these duties.

To prepare for our war time mission, we even reconnoitered the area to locate suitable gun battery positions for use in event of hostilities. After a few months of training, the decision was made to get some practice shooting at aerial targets. The firing range was on the beach about 50 miles north of Tokyo. The gun batteries were sent there, one battery at a time, to conduct their practice.

The Navy supplied us with a search and rescue boat (a reconditioned WW II PT boat). Its purpose was to clear the range area of Japanese fishermen during the firing practice. One night the search and rescue boat's engine stopped working and the boat was being swept towards shore by a strong storm. The crew radioed for help since there were steep rocky cliffs in the area. I was dispatched to the local fishing village to mount a rescue effort.

I contacted the mayor and he agreed to help. The mayor got about 75 villagers to help push their largest fishing boat into the bay. The boat was about 45-50 feet long, 10-15 feet wide, had a diesel engine, and was constructed of heavy wood planking. It had a crew of about 10. We got the engine started and put out to sea. The engine was an old, primitive one cylinder diesel engine. To start the engine, the whole cylinder head was covered with a heavy coating of tallow and then set afire. When cylinder became red hot, the crank was turned and the engine started; pop, pop, pop.........

The sea was very rough, and I spent most of the time trying to keep my stomach in place. We searched almost the whole night and did not find the boat. We returned to the bay and the same 75 men dragged the boat up onto shore.

We went to the mayor's house and were informed that the search and rescue boat had just been found. Luckily, it was washed ashore on one of the few sandy beaches in the area. It was sitting on shore about 100 feet inland. The mayor treated us to 3 or 4 small cups of hot sake and some crunchy snacks. The refreshments really made us feel a lot better.

As we were leaving, I asked what were those tasty little snacks. He said they were "fried grasshoppers."

I agreed with the Army that it was time for me and the family to be returned to the States.

CHAPTER 10

MILITARY ASSIGNMENTS - UNITED STATES

Preface:

The family returned to the United States from Japan in February, 1949. My assignments were of a routine nature. However, events of major importance were taking place throughout the world.

The rebuilding of our Armed Forces was proceeding at an accelerated pace. The Soviet Union exploded their first atomic bomb. North Korea invaded South Korea. The spread of Soviet Communism was proceeding at an alarming rate.

Our State Department announced that South Korea was no longer within our zone of concern. The response of North Korea was to immediately invade South Korea. President Truman reacted quickly and committed US troops to the defense of South Korea. After some initial reverses, The US and Allied forces regained the initiative and pushed the North Korean forces all the way to the Yalu River on the Chinese border,

However, at this point the Chinese launched their massive surprise attack with hundreds of thousands of so called "volunteers." Initially, it had great success. Then, the Allies launched their counter offensive. It was so successful that the Chinese "volunteers" began retreating in disorder. They were surrendering "en masse," as many as 10,000 in a day. There were so many POW's that the Allies had to pull an entire combat division out of the line just to take care of the prisoners.

The Chinese immediately asked for "peace talks." Instead of continuing the offensive during the talks, the Allied Forces were ordered to halt. The Chinese, master negotiators, attained at the peace table what they could not gain on the battle field. Even the most amateurish of military minds would have insisted on a demarcation line that was in our favor, for example, the narrowest part of the peninsula in North Korea, such as from Pyongyang to Wonsan.

Many thought that President Truman fired the wrong person, MacArthur. They felt that instead he should have cleaned out the State Department and their ideological sympathizers. Had he done so, the history of the Far East might have been quite different, especially as concerns a nuclear equipped North Korea and maybe Vietnam.

It is a small wonder that at this point there were some who believed that without outside help, the State Department could not have been so inept or disingenuous. The turmoil that followed was not pleasant.

However, this chapter will be limited to only those incidents in which the author was personally involved.

Fort Bliss, Texas
Fort George G. Meade, Maryland
Fort Sill, Oklahoma
Stewart AFB, New York

Fort Bliss, Texas:

Upon returning to the States, I was assigned to Fort Bliss, the home of Antiaircraft Artillery. Since this was only a temporary assignment, the family remained in New York, while I went to Fort Bliss.

At that time, the Soviet Union enjoyed a large superiority over the United States in numbers of combat aircraft. Therefore, antiaircraft artillery was given a high priority in the rapid expansion of the Army. About ten battalions were being reactivated and trained at Fort Bliss. While there, two happenings took place, which affected my future in the Army in a positive manner. Again, it appeared that I had a little help from above.

The first was my assignment as a battery commander in a 90mm gun battalion. In all modesty, I was one of the most knowledgeable officers in the Army concerning the 90mm antiaircraft gun. I had written a number of articles concerning the gun, which were published in the Antiaircraft Journal. There was little about the gun that I myself developed or discovered. My knowledge was mostly a compilation of "lessons learned" during World War II. I was surprised to see how few WW II antiaircraft officers remembered these lessons. (Photo Page 85)

Specifically, these lessons learned concerned the orientation/ synchronization of the guns, radar, and computer, as well as the meticulous training of the gun crews. Orientation refers to the mechanical alignment of the equipment, and synchronization refers to the electrical alignment of the guns, radar, and computer. Once these procedures are done correctly, then it is a relatively simple matter to apply other gunnery factors, such as, muzzle velocity, air temperature, humidity, winds aloft, powder temperature, weight of projectile, and geographic offset. When the above are done correctly, the 90mm gun will consistently hit the intended target.

As a result of applying the above factors, my battery was not only the best firing battery in the battalion, but also in all of Fort Bliss. It raised the reputation of the whole battalion as well. I was honored by being appointed to the Fort Bliss testing team. Our job was to examine the other battalions to determine if they had completed their training successfully and were ready to be deployed in the field.

The second happening during this period was my application for an appointment into the Regular Army as a Second Lieutenant. The Post WW II Army had an abundance of officers but a serious shortage of Second Lieutenants. This was one time that my age (28) was of benefit, but my lack of any college education was a handicap. The application featured a one year "competitive tour," during which I received various assignments, and my performance was evaluated carefully by four senior officers. With my assignment to a 90mm gun battalion, my acceptance was a "shoo-in."

As a Second Lieutenant in the Regular Army, I was permitted to retain my temporary rank as a captain. Although I lost about 8 years of seniority, there were many other benefits. No longer could I be dismissed at the whim of a superior officer. Further, my career would be carefully monitored so that I received appropriate assignments and schooling to fully round out my military career.

As a sidelight to my tour of duty at Fort Bliss, I was a little sad to find that the old Officers Club was replaced by a new one. The old one was destroyed by fire. Most disheartening was the fact that also destroyed was one of the most famous paintings of "Custer's Last Fight" see photo. It was about 9 feet high, 16 feet wide and was painted by Cassilly Adams. Today, it would be worth millions. Adolphus Busch Sr., paid $35,000 for it in 1892. It had been on display at the Fort Bliss Officers Club in honor of General Custer because Fort Bliss had been the home of one of the last Cavalry Regiments in the US Army. The regiment had been used in our unsuccessful effort to capture Pancho Villa.

CUSTER'S LAST FIGHT

(Painting by Cassilly Adams)

Also interesting was the situation at the boarder check point on the bridge between El Paso and Juarez, Mexico. El Paso was a typical sleepy western city of modest size. Its main source of income was Fort Bliss and Webb Air Force Base. Juarez was a typical "tourist trap." Because of the existing exchange rates, it was an inexpensive tourist trap, scotch and soda 15 cents. At that time, Americans were allowed to bring one bottle of liquor per person, duty free into the US each month. I knew one individual who would carry his six month old baby with him into Mexico and return with two bottles. According to the law, the baby was classified as a "person."

It was odd that the liquor was declared duty free by the federal government, but the State of Texas would collect a modest import duty on the bottle. Texas had been an independent nation when it joined the Union, and it seems that this was one privilege they retained for themselves. It is the only state so privileged.

Another feature of that era was the radio station in nearby Clint, Texas. It claimed to be the most powerful radio station in the nation. It covered all of central United States and could be heard as far north as Ohio. It played only country and western music. Actually, the only part of the station that was in Clint, Texas was their mail box. The large antenna array was across the boarder in Mexico, where regulations concerning radio frequencies and the power used were very relaxed. At the time, it was one of my favorite stations. It kept me alert while traveling by auto over long distances.

Probably my most interesting experience occurred in the Fort Bliss movie theater. One evening while I was waiting for the movie to begin, I heard the couple behind me speaking German. They were in civilian clothes and nicely dressed. I found out later that they were part of the Wernher von Braun team of missile scientists who were secretly brought over from Germany to the United States after World II. The entire station hospital complex of Fort Bliss was converted into a secret compound to house the scientists and their families. Their job was to aid the Army with its missile program at the White Sands Proving Grounds. Once the Berlin Blockade started, the secrecy was lifted and they were free to roam about the base.

Later, the missile scientist were moved to the Army's Redstone Arsenal at Huntsville, Alabama. It was there that they achieved everlasting fame with the Apollo Moon Program.

At the completion of our training, the battalion was transferred to our permanent station at Fort Meade, Maryland. There, I was joined by the family and after a modest delay, we were assigned comfortable family living quarters on the post.

Fort George G. Meade:

Our arrival at Fort Meade was uneventful. The post was named after the Commander of the victorious Union Forces at Gettysburg, General George G. Meade. Not being very flamboyant, his role in the battle was diminished by most historians.

Our mission was to provide antiaircraft protection to the Capitol, should the need arise. We would move into pre-selected sites in the event of an emergency. In the meantime, we would continue our training. Our practice firing range was out over the ocean, between Ocean City, Maryland, and Rehoboth, Delaware.

I was the Plans and Operations Officer for the battalion, and it was not long before I committed my first boo-boo. I went on a reconnaissance of the Capitol area to pre-select gun sites for use if, and when required. A few days later, our Brigade Headquarters wanted to know what blockhead selected the site in the Northeast quadrant of Washington. Directly across the boulevard, and in the center of the expected field of fire, was the 20 story high

Bethesda Naval Hospital. The tall building would make it impossible for the radars and guns to cover that sector properly.

Of course, I was the person responsible. The gun site itself was in a nice lawn covered area in the corner of a golf course. It was wide open and appeared to have an unobstructed field of fire. The weather on the day of reconnaissance was light rain with a heavy fog. I did not see the 20 story high Bethesda Naval Hospital across the boulevard. Needless to say, I never again conducted a reconnaissance in foggy weather.

My reputation was partly redeemed later when I handled our move to and from the Army's annual maneuvers at Fort Bragg, North Carolina. It was then that next major event for the Genero family took place. Our son, Mark, was born at the Fort Meade Station Hospital.

The Korean War began about this time. Since we had such an important stateside mission, our battalion was not considered for deployment to the Far East. However, I personally tried to volunteer for a Korean assignment. The Army promised that if I was sent to Korea, they would continue to provide comfortable living quarters for the family on the post. Also, we had numerous friends on the post who would assist the family, should the need arise.

I got into our car and headed for the Pentagon to see the personnel officer and volunteer for Korean duty. I had driven into the District of Columbia less than a mile when a police officer "pulled me over." It seems that my car had license plates, which had just expired. The new plates had not yet arrived. The police officer gave me an option. Either turn around and return to Fort Meade or receive multiple citations. I opted to turn around and return to Fort Meade. It appeared that once more I was being guided from above and told not to go to Korea.

My commission in the Regular Army was beginning to pay dividends. I was selected to attend the radar/computer school at the Aberdeen Proving Grounds in Maryland. It was close enough so that I could come home for the weekends. I did reasonably well, but there was one phase that did give me a little problem. It was "circuit tracing." There were sheets upon sheets of wiring diagrams, and one was expected to trace a signal through pages and pages of them. My answers were always close but often incorrect. On the final examination, I decided to try an experiment. There were about six such problems. After carefully tracing the signals through a number of components, I would arrive at an answer, On the answer sheet, I wrote in exactly the opposite of what I had determined. It was the correct answer three out of the six times.

One of our most unusual problems took place, while we were on maneuvers, occupying our tactical site around Washington. It was winter and unusually cold. The District parks commissioner had supplied us with complete latrine facilities, which were housed in an aluminum trailer. It was so cold that the water pipes were freezing overnight. Our solution was to detail a soldier to remain in the trailer and to open the faucets and flush the commodes every five minutes. It worked, but the soldier performing this duty was less than thrilled at this extra curricular assignment.

Finally, there was a little "fun" incident. Our group Commander was an extreme "worry wart." Nothing escaped his attention, even the most minute detail. He worried constantly about what higher headquarters was thinking of his performance. On one occasion, while we were on maneuvers, our Brigade Headquarters sent an inspection team to evaluate our performance. One member of the team was one of my oldest and best buddies. He was one of the best radar officers in the Army. During the inspection, I noticed that my buddy was making copious notes.

As he was leaving, I asked him what was in all of the notes he was making. He showed his notebook. Page after page contained nothing but his name, written over and over again. He explained that every time he noticed that the Group Commander was looking in his direction, he would take out his note book and pretend to be making notes on how the group was performing. We both wondered on how many hours of sleep the Group Commander lost, worrying about what was going to be reported to the Brigade Commander. Naturally, we passed inspection quite comfortably.

In the summer of 1951, my career development officer in the Pentagon, selected me to attend the year long Artillery Officer's Course at Fort Sill, Oklahoma and Fort Bliss, Texas.

The Artillery School, Fort Sill and Fort Bliss:

The school was a full year of instruction on all types of artillery and its use in every conceivable situation, in all possible climates and in every foreseeable geographic location. Three months were spent at Fort Bliss for instruction on antiaircraft weapons.

We were sorry to hear that there was no post housing available at Fort Sill for the families of the students. We bought a small house in the nearby city of Lawton. By today's standard, the purchase of the house was unbelievably easy. We simply signed the back of the deed and recorded it in the county clerk's office. It took only 20 minutes. The total cost was the $15 registration fee.

At Fort Sill, the most famous building was the Geronimo Museum. It was the building in which he was imprisoned and from which he made his famous escape, see photo. Fort Sill was also a buffalo sanctuary, and the buffalo were making a strong comeback.

OLD GERONIMO GUARD HOUSE BUILT 1871-1872

The studies were not too difficult, and we spent our out of class time participating in various sports programs. I was catcher on our softball team. We did well but won no trophies.

Living conditions off post were tolerable but not exceedingly comfortable. One night around midnight we even had a tornado touch ground a couple of blocks from our house. It tore a path of destruction through the neighborhood but did not cause any serious injuries. No one in our family heard a thing.

All was quite routine and there were only a few minor incidents of interest. One was a parachute drop demonstrating the powers of an airborne assault. Evidently there was a change of direction in the winds at the last moment. Instead of landing in the drop zone, the paratroopers landed all over the spectators. It was strange to look up and see a multitude of paratroopers landing right on top of us. Luckily there were no serious injuries,

An embarrassing incident happened during one of the combined arms classes at For Still. In one class after lunch, I became drowsy and nodded off. On seeing this, the instructor suddenly called on me for the answer to a question he had just asked and which, of course, I hadn't heard. I jumped up and blurted out the first thing that came to my mind which was, "Forty trucks, Sir!" There was a roar of laughter in the auditorium. From then on, I was known as "Forty-Truck-Pete." To this day, I don't know what prompted me to give such a ridiculous answer.

We were anxious to finish the course and move on to our next assignment and, hopefully, more comfortable living quarters. However, I stayed at Fort Sill for a few more months as I was selected to receive additional training to qualify as a nuclear weapons effects officer. It did not make me happy at that time, but later, I found that the extra training helped me in my future assignments.

Almost as a reward for having to spend the extra time at Fort Sill, my next assignment took us to the Army Eastern Antiaircraft Command at Stewart Air Force Base, New York.

Stewart Air Force Base, New York:

In the fall of 1952, our family arrived at Stewart Air Force Base, New York. It was near West Point, and it served as an auxiliary airfield for the Academy. I was assigned to the Eastern Army Antiaircraft Command, which was co-located with the Air Force, Eastern Air Defense Command.

This was during an intense period of the Cold War. The nation had activated its entire air defense capability. The Navy deployed its "picket ships" along our coasts to provide early warning in event of an attack. The Air Force, with their long range radars and fighter aircraft, provided "area" air defense for the country. The Army provided "point" air defense for key government/ population/industrial centers, such as Washington, New York, Detroit, etc.

As the situation developed, there was not enough room at Stewart AFB to accommodate our command. Therefore, our headquarters and control center was physically located in the nearby city of Middletown. There, we were able to find comfortable living quarters at reasonable rates. All in all, it was a pleasant environment. Also, it was close to our respective families, and there were many mutual visits.

The Eastern Army Antiaircraft Command was in charge of all Army antiaircraft units, that were deployed east of the Mississippi River, about 30 battalions. They were on a 24 hour a day alert status and armed with live ammunition. I was assigned to the Operations Division. My specific duty was to inspect all of our defense sites to determine their readiness. With a few exceptions, they all fulfilled their requirements.

Because of my extensive radar background, I was also the Command's electronic countermeasures (ECM) officer. My main task was to ensure that our radar operators were sufficiently trained to overcome enemy attempts to "jam" our radars.

To aid in our training, the Air Force provided a squadron of airplanes equipped with all sorts of "jamming" equipment and devices. They would fly scheduled missions against our defenses to make our ECM training more realistic. On occasion, I would fly with them to help coordinate their missions. The planes they used were the old venerable B-25 medium bombers of the Doolittle raid on Tokyo.

There were times that I got the feeling that the aircrews were a little uncomfortable with me aboard. Invariably, the aircraft seemed to have problems including emergency landings when I was a passenger. One week we started out with four planes, but had only one in flyable condition at the end of the week. My first awkward "encounter" with military aviation.

Being close to both families, we had many family visits and enjoyed them all. This was the first time in my 12 years of service that we were this close to our families. Our house was a solidly built (pre-WW II) two story house with lots of room. Probably the only drawback was the coal fired furnace for hot water and steam heat. The shoveling of coal and removal of ashes was not my forte.

One of my favorite little gimmicks was to take the male visitors down into the cellar to show them how solidly the house was built, 4 x12 rough cut beams, etc. Of course the cellar was also the store room for the family made wine and distilled rye whiskey. It did not take long for the visiting female members to evaluate the situation and insist that they also be escorted to the cellar to "inspect the beams."

The greatest event during this period was the birth of Peter Jr. at the West Point Station Hospital. It was almost a dramatic event. It so happened that I was away on an inspection trip and my wife, Betty, with our children were visiting my folks at the family homestead in Rosendale. There, the birth pangs began in earnest. My mother simply put Betty in the family car and told my sister Rita to take her to West Point. Before leaving, my mother, being an old hand at this sort of thing, put blankets and sheets in the car, along with a bottle of our family's rye whiskey. However, they made it to the hospital in time, and Peter Jr. joined the Genero family.

As happens in life, all good things must come to and end. In the summer of 1953, I received orders to report immediately to Iceland. It was to be a solo one year tour. The family remained in Middletown, which was not too bad, since so many members of the family were close by. To expedite my arrival in Iceland, I was flown there in an Air Force C-97, a cargo version of the Boeing B-29 Strategic (atom) Bomber.

En route to Iceland and out over the Atlantic Ocean, the plane developed engine trouble. Luckily, the plane could fly well on three engines. We made an emergency landing at Saint John's, Newfoundland. The engine was repaired and the next day we flew on to Iceland. This was my second awkward "encounter" with military aviation.

CHAPTER 11

ICELAND

Preface:

Volumes and volumes could be written about Iceland; it is such an interesting and unique place. However, this preface will be limited to a few geographic facts and Iceland's role in the international political arena.

Iceland is a large island about the size of the state of Virginia, located in the North Atlantic Ocean, see map. It is located about 560 miles northwest of Scotland and about 150 miles southeast of Greenland. Mainly it is covered by glaciers and lava beds. Only about 2% is cultivated, and only about 20 % is fit for grazing.

Iceland's population is about 300,000, of Nordic and Gaelic decent. Ninety-nine percent live in urban areas. Fishing is the dominate industry since it is located in one of the richest fishing grounds of the world. Lately, aluminum has also become one of its chief exports. Iceland is blessed with an abundance of hydro-electric and geo-thermal power. Its capitol, Reykjavik, is heated by natural hot water springs.

Iceland was discovered and settled during the 900's. Its people have been credited by many to have been the original discoverers of North America. It has always been a semi-independent nation with ties to Norway and later Denmark. It has been fully independent since 1918. During World War II, it was invaded by Great Britain to forestall a possible German occupation. In June, 1941 (before Pearl Harbor), the United States landed troops in Iceland and assumed responsibility for its protection. Iceland did not have, nor has today, any armed forces. This US/Icelandic

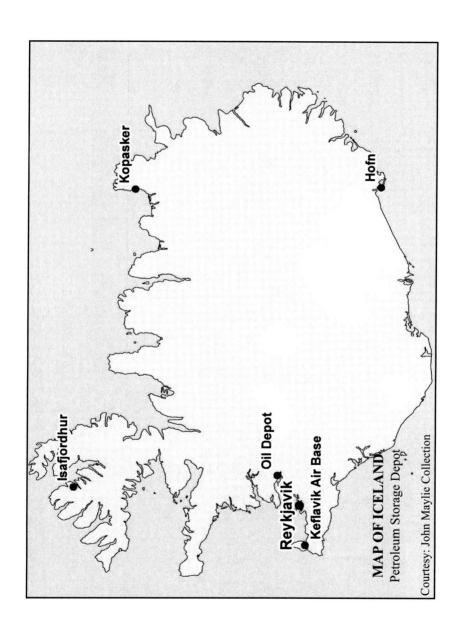

MAP OF ICELAND
Petroleum Storage Depot

Kopasker

Hofn

Isafjordhur

Oil Depot

Reykjavik

Keflavik Air Base

Courtesy: John Maylie Collection

situation continued, in one fashion or another, until March, 2006, when the last of the US Armed Forces withdrew.

Its dominant religion is Lutheran, and its Althing, parliament, is considered to be one of the oldest in the world, dating back to the 900's. Iceland's literacy rate is 99.9%, and its per capita book/magazine rate is the highest in the world.

During the Cold War, Iceland was a key element in the Allied policy of "containment." Whoever controlled Iceland, controlled the North Atlantic. It could almost be described as the cork in the bottle to prevent Soviet expansion into the Western Hemisphere. It was of extreme importance to the defense of the United States. Our radar network there could provide early warning of a Soviet air attack. The long range fighter planes stationed there could intercept Soviet bombers, should they attempt to attack the United States. It was a key element in our world-wide communications network (i.e. before satellites). Finally, the Keflavik Air Force Base was an extremely important refueling base for US retaliatory strikes against the Soviet Union.

For the Navy, Iceland possessed the largest petroleum supply depot in the North Atlantic. Its location made it a critical factor in our anti-submarine campaign. At that time, the Soviets had the largest submarine fleet in the world. Their free access to the Atlantic Ocean had to be curtailed to the maximum extent possible.

Probably the most interesting feature of my tour of duty in Iceland was that my roommate later became an infamous figure in the American domestic political arena.

In summary, the possession of Iceland was critical to the defense of the free world and especially the United States.

The Iceland Defense Force
George Lincoln Rockwell

Iceland Defense Force (IDF)

The Iceland Defense Force (IDF) was a Joint (Army, Navy, Air Force) US Command responsible for protecting Iceland from foreign occupation. There was a fairly strong Communist party in Iceland. Together with the Socialist, they exerted a major influence in Icelandic politics. In addition, there was a very large Soviet fishing fleet constantly operating in Icelandic waters. A significant landing force could be put ashore, at will. Together with their Icelandic political allies, the Soviets could peacefully assume control of Iceland.

Arriving at the Keflavik International Airport, I was a solitary figure, with my bags, looking for assistance. I located a Military Police desk and asked their help. I informed them that I was Major Genero, assigned to IDF, and needed transportation. They so informed IDF Headquarters.

A few minutes later, a military staff car, with escort and sirens blaring, roared up to the terminal. A Colonel jumped out and went racing up and down the terminal, evidently seeking someone. He found me and asked if I had seen a "Major General" looking for transportation. I then realized that the Military Police phone call to IDF Headquarters had been misunderstood. They had mistakenly taken Major Genero to mean Major General.

The Colonel turned out to be my boss. That evening, after a welcoming cocktail, we all had a few laughs over the incident.

My assignment to the joint staff was as a plans and operations officer. My specific job was to establish an antiaircraft defense for the enormous petroleum storage depot near Reykjavik.

It was the most important refueling depot in the entire North Atlantic. Without it, neither our Navy nor the NATO Navy could operate effectively in that area. Further, our Air Force units, which were stationed there, would not have been able to carry out their assigned missions.

There was an antiaircraft battalion at Fort Bliss, Texas, specifically designated and trained for this mission. The battalion was equipped with the Skysweeper, see photo. It was the newest antiaircraft gun in our arsenal. It was a rapid fire 75mm gun with its own individual radar and computer. Our first task was to obtain permission from the Icelandic Government for the deployment of this battalion. Needless to say, with the Communist influence in their government, permission was never obtained.

Courtesy: Air Defense Artillery Museum. Fort Bliss, TX

SKYSWEEPER 75 MM ANTICRAFT GUN

My staff duties became routine. We constantly analyzed the Soviet threat, especially the activities of their fishing fleet. Our plans for the ground defense of the Keflavik Airport were being reviewed and updated on a daily basis. Also, I monitored the installation of the Air Force's new long range radars, which were being installed on the four corners of Iceland. Except for the Hofn radar,this responsibility led to a couple of interesting situations.

I was visiting the radar site in the Isafjordhur area, (northwest corner), when the weather turned bad. We had arrived by Icelandic (seaplane) Airline and landed in the fjord. The weather became too severe for the seaplane to take off and it kept blowing hard for three days. We were treated royally by the local inhabitants in a nearby small fishing village. The food was excellent. The accommodations were spotless. The "down" comforter and pillows made sleeping an ultimate pleasure. We were almost sorry to leave. The hostel was owned and operated by the "Salvation Army." It has been one of my favorite charities ever since.

A short while later, I had my third awkward "encounter" with military aviation. It took place when our inspection team flew, via Navy PBY flying boat, to the Kopasker area on the Northeast corner of Iceland. Before we could disembark, a sudden Artic storm descended upon the bay. The rudder of the seaplane became jammed, and we could not take off. The waves were breaking over the seaplane, and we were in danger of sinking. The pilot, by using the power of the engines, was able to steer the plane towards the rocky shore. It got hung up on a large rocky ledge which prevented us from sinking. We stayed there until the storm subsided. A small open dory evacuated us to shore. The one other item I remembered about the trip was that the baked fresh cod fish served at the American construction site was the finest tasting cod fish that I have ever had.

We returned to Keflavik via a small Icelandic coastal steamer. It was a strange feeling to be lifted aboard ship by means of a cargo net. There were no docks or piers to facilitate loading the ship. Again, the accommodations were spotless and the food was both excellent and plentiful. However, the food did require a taste for fish. At one meal, we were served "seven" varieties of seafood.

Of course we participated in "the required event" for all American visitors to Iceland. During the continuous daylight of summer, we played a "midnight softball game."

The University of Maryland conducted extension courses in Iceland. It helped pass the time during the long winter nights and permitted me to earn credits towards my degree.

Our IDF Headquarters was housed in a windowless domed hutment. In the winter, we would enter in the morning (dark); come out for lunch (light); and then re-emerge in the evening (dark). This led me to perhaps my biggest boo-boo in Iceland.

One winter day I was requested to inspect the artillery units in Iceland to determine their combat readiness. The inspection was scheduled for a Saturday morning, and I was asked what time I would like to conduct the inspection. I told them, "At 9 AM." I did not realize that at 9AM it was still dark. Upon making this discovery and after I regained my composure, I simply asked for a powerful flashlight and conducted the inspection as scheduled.

Next to the petroleum storage depot was a whaling station. It was an interesting operation. There were about a dozen whaling boats at the station. They were small in size. The boats were about the size of the standard tug boat in New York harbor. Each had a very high bow, upon which was mounted a harpoon gun. Once the whale was caught, it was tied to the boat, tail first, and towed up the fjord to the whaling station. It was not unusual to see two whales being towed by a single boat. During the season, the station would handle 6 to 10 whales per day.

The station was a large factory type building, about 20-30 feet above water level, with a wide concrete ramp going from the factory down into the water. The tail of the whale would be attached to a winch and the whale would be pulled slowly up the ramp into the factory. Along the ramp, there would be a team of about a dozen men with long handled, very sharp, cutting blades, similar to a machete. They would hack off specific parts and deposit them in assigned subterranean vats for further processing. In less than an hour, the entire whale was disected.

Of course while there, I had to eat whale meat for lunch. It was not too bad, especially if sprinkled with enough seasoning. The only problem was that the powerful odious smell of whale blubber seemed to remain with me for a couple of days.

One of the most magnificent sights that I have ever seen was the aurora borealis (Northern Lights) swishing across the sky on a dark clear night over Iceland. They appeared to be a flow of multicolored cloud-like formations traveling across the sky, horizon to horizon. They were constantly changing colors, sizes and shapes as they traveled across the sky. Particularly enchanting was the manner in which they would "whip" through the atmosphere. I don't know whether it is scientifically correct or not, but I will insist till my dying day that I could actually hear the swishing and snapping sounds of the lights as they passed overhead. Of course some of my companions claimed that it was only the after effects of that fine Tuborg beer, which was served at the Officers Club.

At the end of my tour of duty in Iceland, I was assigned to the Army Antiaircraft Command Headquarters at Colorado Springs, one of the most pleasant areas of our country.

George Lincoln Rockwell:

It may be surprising to the reader to find a complete section of my reminiscences devoted to George Lincoln Rockwell. However, we shared a tiny apartment in Keflavik for almost a complete year.

I was completely dumbfounded when eight years later I found out that he had become the leader of the American Nazi Party. I scrupulously avoided any contact (phone, visit, meeting etc.) with him, even though he lived close to me in Arlington, Virginia. I not only had no use for the Nazi party, but I did not want to compromise my highly sensitive position in the Pentagon.

Rockwell was a naval reserve officer (pilot), called back to active duty during the Korean War. He was sent to Iceland because of his background in anti-submarine warfare.

I tried to analyze our association and comprehend how or why he "went off the deep end," and became the leader of such an intolerable movement. The following is a summary of my views on the subject,

While sharing our apartment, I had many discussions and dealings with Rockwell. During that period, he never indicated any extremist views or sympathies. Of course, he had the normal respect for military discipline and authority. His manner was always thoughtful, correct, and considerate.

After World War II, he became a commercial artist and illustrator. As I recall, he also indicated that he had been the editor of a small publication in New England. I found him to be one of the most knowledgeable persons that I had ever met. He could discuss almost any subject thoughtfully and with meaningful observations. To be frank, at times I was awed by his knowledge and analysis of events.

As an example of the above, he taught himself to read, write, and speak the Icelandic language within six months. He was so proficient that often he was used as an interpreter. He was one of the few Americans who had free and easy access to Reykjavik. The rest of us service personnel were restricted to Keflavik. He was so well received by the Icelandic people that he mingled freely with local leaders and government officials. It was in this environment that he met and married the daughter of the Icelandic Ambassador to the United States.

When my tour of duty in Iceland was completed, I returned to the United States. Rockwell chose to remain in Iceland. During the long winter nights in Iceland, a person has ample time to reflect on many things. I believe that it was during this transitional period that he developed his extremist views.

He wanted to transform the economy and culture of the United States into a utopian community similar to Iceland. Before one ridicules and dismisses the idea that Iceland is a utopia, let me explain.

There are no super rich (Donald Trump style) people, or extremely poor (beggars, homeless, destitute, hungry) people in Iceland. Every person has adequate food, clothing and shelter. They have a wealthy class, but they are not ostentatiously so. Everyone has at least a modest home, proper clothing, sufficient food, free medical care, good education, and is gainfully employed. There are no "shanty" towns or "slum" areas. All houses are comfortable and solidly built. It was the first time that I ever heard of "a hundred year home mortgage."

Because of the harsh climate, proper clothing was essential. Their clothing always appeared to be neat, comfortable, and suitable for the activity in which they are engaged. However, it was not carried to extremes. I had never heard of an Icelander owning 50 suits, dresses, or pairs of shoes.

There were no perennial loafers on the streets. It almost appeared as if they had taken the words of Saint Paul literally. [II Thessalonians, 2:10, "if any man not work, neither let him eat"]

The people seemed to take pride in their jobs whether it was cutting up a whale, working in a canning factory, or sitting behind a desk in a bank. Everyone had the equivalent of at least a high school education.

They have a non-alcoholic and virtual crime free society. Iceland has no armed forces, and their police are not armed. They have only a few light weapons in the country, which are stored in a warehouse. The Chief of Police is reputed to have the only key. Even their Coast Guard is not armed.

There was one incident in which a group of American construction workers decided to test the capabilities of the Icelandic unarmed police. It was during one of their Saturday night melees. The next morning the ring leaders appeared before the local magistrate. One had a broken arm, and the other one had a dislocated shoulder.

Their nominal religion is Lutheran. In fact, the local bishop was the uncle of the bride who married George Lincoln Rockwell. They have a tiny Catholic congregation, but no synagogue.

Their culture seems immersed in fine poetry, classic literature, traditional art, and classical music. These cultural fields are almost worshipped. As an example, Marian Anderson, the famous black American soprano, gave a concert in Reykjavik; the entire country was euphoric and could not give her enough praise. This was despite the fact that blacks are not permitted to live in Iceland. The Embassy scheduled her performance to demonstrate how talented blacks were in the classic arts.

Athletics are highly regarded. There are many gymnasiums and heated indoor swimming pools. One of their favorite outdoor activities is hiking or taking long walks. It is not unusual to see scores of people, especially seniors, taking a stroll up and down the streets of Reykjavik at 11 or 12 PM during a bright summer's night. As a matter of interest, I never saw an obese person in Iceland.

It might be mentioned that the Armed Forces Radio station at Keflavik had to operate at a very low level of power. The Icelanders did not want us Americans to contaminate their culture.

It is my feeling that George Lincoln Rockwell wanted to convert the American economy and culture into a similar utopian nation and society. However, first he had to segregate the blacks (give them their own country) and insure that the Jews were not in any positions of authority. He was assassinated in December, 1967, apparently over an internal party dispute.

It might be mentioned that the United States seems to have adopted one of the features of the Icelandic culture in a very prolific manner, without the benefit of George Lincoln Rockwell. In 1952, the parents of one third of all the children born in Iceland were not married. In polite circles, it was called "Trial Marriage."

CHAPTER 12

NORTH AMERICAN AIROSPACE DEFENSE COMMAND (NORAD)

Preface:

I was assigned to the Army Air Defense Command (ARADCOM) at Ent Air Force Base in Colorado Springs, Colorado.

Ent was a small base about the size of a college campus, situated by itself in a residential area of the city. Its airfield was at Peterson AFB, about 5 miles out on the flats away from Pikes Peak. The unique feature of Ent was that a large solid concrete building called the Blockhouse was located on the base. It served as the operations center for NORAD. Later, the center was moved into a bomb proof cave dug into the base of nearby Cheyenne Mountain.

NORAD was a joint (Army, Navy, Air Force) command responsible for the air defense of North America. It was commanded by General Partridge, USAF. This was during an intense period of the Cold War. The Soviet Union not only had the atom bomb, but also intercontinental bombers capable of delivering them to the United States. This was before the advent of intercontinental ballistic missiles.

The Air Force had the primary responsibility for the "area" air defense of the United States. They had the United States covered with radars and fighter interceptors on constant alert (airborne within 3 minutes). They also had the famous Distant Early Warning (DEW) Line. This was a chain of long range radars stretching from Alaska, across Northern Canada, to Greenland and Iceland.

The Navy had "picket ships" along both coasts to provide early warning of a possible air attack using a sea approach. They were also deeply concerned with the Soviet submarine threat. In addition, they could provide limited air defense of their naval installations located in the United States.

ARADCOM, Lieutenant General Mickelsen commanding, was the Army element of NORAD. It provided "point" air defense for the major population/industrial centers, such as Washington, New York, Chicago, Detroit and Los Angeles. For the Army, this was the period of transition from guns to guided missiles.

Such was the "big picture" of the air defense of the United States during the 1954 - 1957 period.

Colorado Springs
The Block House
Unidentified Flying Objects (UFO's)

Colorado Springs:

I flew back to the United States in relative comfort. It was in an Air Force plane configured for passenger travel However, for some strange reason all of our seats were facing to the rear.

Upon arrival in the States, our first task was to clear customs. The lines were long and slow moving. I noticed that the customs official handling our line was very strict. Suddenly, I realized that the scotch I was carrying was in an "imperial quart" bottle. It was a little larger than the allowable US quart bottle. I was concerned that the stern customs official might have it confiscated. I finally thought of a solution. I opened the bottle and drank the excess ounces. I passed inspection with no problems and proceeded on my way.

It's strange, but there was one factor which caught my attention as I was going through the air terminal building. There appeared to be quite a number of people walking around the terminal who were obese, and there were many others dressed in less than a neat manner. It was a dramatic change from what I had witnessed in Iceland.

I picked up the family in Middletown, NY, and we drove to Colorado Springs. Since there were no family quarters on the base, we had to live in the surrounding community. Our modest house was comfortable and the local people were friendly and cooperative. The view of Pikes Peak was quite impressive. It was snow capped almost all year. One year we went to the summit on the 4th of July and threw snow balls at one another.

Another interesting event was the spectacular fireworks display that would take place on Pikes Peak each New Years Eve. It could be seen for fifty miles. It was started by Lowell Thomas, a very popular radio newscaster and world traveler. Their organization was called the Add-A-Man Club. It was so named because only one new number was permitted to join each year. They would climb up the mountain and put on the fireworks display each New Years Eve.

The Garden of the Gods which is located at the base of Pikes Peak is a beautiful park and ideal for family picnics. Our family took advantage of it quite often.

As could be expected, there were several severe snow storms in Colorado Springs. Three feet of snow was not unusual. At times, only those with skies and I could get around the city. As a second car, I had an old 1936 NASH, which was built quite high off the ground. With chains, it was virtually unstoppable, even in deep snow.

Speaking of cars, we participated in one related event. One

Thanksgiving we did not have a turkey. We read in the newspaper that a De Soto automobile dealer would give a free turkey to anyone who bought a new De Soto. Yep! We bought a new De Soto and got a free turkey, which we enjoyed on Thanksgiving Day.

One of my most intriguing experiences in Colorado concerned fishing. Often at the movies, there would be clips showing President Eisenhower fishing in some of the inviting lakes and streams of Colorado and catching a mess of fish. Seizing the opportunity, I bought some fishing gear and went fishing.

The lakes and streams were beautiful. If I were a fish, it's where I would live and swim. However, it did not turn out as I had expected. After several weeks, all that I managed to catch was one little trout, about 7 - 8 inches in length.

Some time later I was at a cocktail party and happened to meet the Colorado Fish and Game Commissioner. I asked him how could President Eisenhower always catch a mess of fish and I couldn't. After a few more cocktails, he told me the story.

It seems that about two weeks before the president's arrival, the Secret Service would reconnoiter a few possible fishing sites for the President. For security purposes they would not divulge the site selected. The Commissioner, knowing the sites visited, would immediately "stock" each site with hatchery fish. He explained that it took about a week for the hatchery fish to lose their lethargic hatchery habits. They would become frisky and bite on almost anything.

The two week lead time for the president's visit was just about perfect, and he would always catch a mess of fish. The free publicity that these news reel shots of the President catching fish, was invaluable to the Colorado tourist industry.

There was also another incident that I will always remember. The day before Christmas, the Officers Club would have a complimentary eggnog party. Naturally I would avail myself of the opportunity to begin the holidays in the right spirit. While at the party one year, I heard a tremendous crash. It sounded as if a thousand glasses were suddenly smashed.

We rushed to the storeroom to see what happened, One wall of the store-room was lined with shelves on which were stored about a thousand glasses. Protruding into the storeroom, where the glasses were stored, was the front end of a brand new Oldsmobile. It broke through the wall and smashed almost all the glasses. It appears that one of the wives, while at the club, sampled (?) the eggnog. She went out to her car to drive home. Since the car was new, she was confused and shifted it into the wrong gear. When she stepped on the gas, the car went forward instead of backward. As happens sometimes, she did not suffer a scratch.

In summary, Colorado Springs was a pleasant place in which to live. I often thought that I would like to retire there. I retained that thought for many years. That was until I made the wrong turn on I-95 and wound up in Florida.

Blockhouse:

At the Army Air Defense Command (ARADCOM), I was assigned as an operations officer. Specifically, I had to monitor and report on the operational status of all deployed Army antiaircraft batteries (200+) in the United States. This was accomplished by means of daily reports and visits to the field. I was also the radar officer. Electronic countermeasures (ECM) was one of our primary concerns.

For some strange reason, I got involved in public speaking. It seems that often there were requests (chambers of commerce, fraternal organizations, schools, etc.) for a speaker, concerning the Army's role in the air defense of the United States. Invariably, I would be selected as the designated speaker. I guess the other staff officers didn't relish the task. Actually, these public speaking engagements, led to what I believe was my most important role in ARADCOM.

I became the Army's liaison officer to NORAD, with a designated operations desk in the "blockhouse," see photos below.

C
O
M
M
A
N
D
E
R
S

B
O
O
T
H

O
P
E
R
A
T
I
O
N
S

O
F
F
I
C
E
R
S

Courtesy: North American Aerospace Defense Command (NORAD)
Colorado Springs, CO
BLOCKHOUSE INTERIOR

The blockhouse was a windowless concrete structure about 100'L x 50' W and 30'H. It contained a large plexiglass plotting board about 20'H x 40'W, flanked by two auxiliary plotting boards. The main plotting board was considered to be the largest sheet of plexiglass in the world. The location of any enemy threat, unknown plane, etc., was plotted manually on those boards. The plotters were stationed on scaffolds in the rear of the board. They used colored crayons and had to learn how to write backwards. Since the lights in the operations center were dimmed, and the plastic boards had "edge lighting", the plots were clearly visible and easily read. Between the commander's booth and the display boards, there were two dais levels with a total of about 30 operations officers. Each had a console and a communications capability with subordinate units. The reader is reminded that this was 50+ years ago, before the age of digital computers and electronic displays.

Each morning I had to brief General Partridge (NORAD Commander) and his staff on the operational status of the Army antiaircraft units deployed to defend our population and industrial centers. At that time we were replacing our antiaircraft gun battalions with NIKE-AJAX guided missile battalions, see photo.

NIKE-AJAX

Courtesy: Air Defense Artillery Museum Fort Bliss, TX

My position was on the second level just below the NORAD Commander. Since his booth was not completely sound proof, I was privy to what was spoken by the various commanders and their assistants. As a result, I was able to understand more fully the significance of a number of events.

The first incident took place on Christmas Eve shortly after my assignment to the blockhouse. I was watching the plotting board and noticed that there was a plot of an unidentified object originating near the North Pole. I further noticed that the plot appeared to be moving toward the United States. Since over-the-pole was the shortest route for Soviet bombers to reach the US, I began paying more attention to it. I noticed that the other operations officers were showing no concerns. When it approached the US boarder, the object was identified. It was a man in a red suit in a sleigh being pulled by six raindeer. The center went to the extent of making hourly public announcements of an unidentified object approaching the US. It was carried by radios all over the country.

I was present during most of the joint exercises that were conducted to test the capability of NORAD to intercept all incoming targets. I can't recall of any instance in which the attacking planes (simulated by Strategic Air Command bombers) failed to be detected. During our post attack analysis, I noticed that the Strategic Air Command plots of their planes seemed to always be 30 to 40 miles from our plots of the same planes. I knew that there must be some mistake because our radars could place a target within 10 yards of its exact location.

As the ARADCOM radar officer, I requested permission to fly in one of their incoming planes during the next exercise. I had hoped that if I could be with their navigator, I could help solve the problem. However, the Strategic Air Command refused permission with the flimsy excuse that I was not trained to wear an oxygen mask at high altitudes. Training to do so would take all of about two hours.

During one exercise, we knew exactly the number of Strategic Air Command bombers, where the planes were, when they would attack, and from what direction their simulated attack on the United States would come.

It was all accomplished by means of radio intercept. In order to refuel their planes while in flight, the pilot of the bomber being refueled had to communicate with the boom operator of the refueling plane They did so by means of radio. All radio transmissions are subject to intercept. By triangulation, we knew where the planes were. By listening to the intercept, we knew how much fuel was taken aboard. From these two factors, we could fairly well predict, where, when, and from what direction the attack was coming. When General LeMay, the commander of the Strategic Air Command, heard that his air crews talked too much over radio, he was furious.

During my tour of duty in the blockhouse, there was one incident which caused all of us severe anxiety. The long range radars on the DEW Line detected a number of unidentified planes off the coast of Alaska headed towards the United States. The NORAD staff contacted all possible agencies to try and identify the planes. When that failed, General Partridge and the other service commanders were notified, and they came to the blockhouse.

I could hear General Partridge informing the White House Staff and other concerned Federal Agencies. He called the CIA, FBI and the heads of all the military intelligence organizations. He was asking each one if they had detected any indication that the Soviets might launch an attack against the United States. They all gave negative reports. However, faced with fact that the unidentified planes were still proceeding towards the United States, he was forced to declare a "Yellow" alert for the Northwest region of the United States.

All states and local civil defense agencies in that area were placed on a high state of alert. Air raid wardens were called to active duty. Fire rescue and relief units were placed on a high state of readiness. Hospitals began preparing for the receipt of a massive number of casualties. Even individual citizens began reviewing their needs for personal air raid shelters.

Air Force fighter interceptors were fueled, armed and dispatched to their assigned sectors. Their back-up interceptors were fueled, armed and placed in a ready status (airborne in 3 minutes). Probably most dramatic of all, plan SCATER was implemented. This meant that all non military aircraft were immediately grounded. Only planes under direct control of military air controllers were permitted in the air.

All Army antiaircraft units were placed on maximum alert. Guided missiles were taken from their underground bunkers, placed on their launching rails, and elevated to their firing positions. The safety pins were exposed so that they could be removed without delay and free the missiles for instant launching.

In the meantime, the unidentified planes were getting closer and closer to the United States. It was reaching the point where General Partridge would have to declare condition "Red" (permission to open fire and destroy the unidentified aircraft).

It was at this point that General LeMay sheepishly admitted that the planes were his. The whole situation gave the appearance that General LeMay was trying to sneak his planes into the United States without being detected. His attempts to do so during scheduled exercises were not successful, so he was trying to do so surreptitiously.

A person of lesser stature would have been promptly disciplined. However, General LeMay (the George Patton of the Air Force) was considered by some to be in the same class as a deity. Once, when asked by a reporter if he got ulcers from his awesome responsibilities. He replied, "I don't get ulcers. I give ulcers." Later, when George Wallace ran for President, he picked General LeMay to be his running mate.

Unidentified Flying Objects (UFO's):

UFO's presented NORAD with a very interesting situation. Were they real? Were they imaginary? Or, were they products of new scientific breakthroughs by the Soviet Union?

NORAD was so concerned that they organized special research teams of technicians, engineers and scientists, to thoroughly examine every report of a UFO. For convenience purposes, the UFO's will be placed into three general categories: radar sightings, recovery of physical objects and visual sightings.

Radar sightings: These were actual radar return signals, which showed up on radar screens as targets. These were the early days of radar, and the propagation of radar waves was still not fully understood. They varied with the prevailing conditions of the troposphere, ionosphere, and even heavy cloud covers. The radar frequencies used were also an important factors in radar responses.

Every unusual radar response was carefully studied. The root causes of almost all were resolved after careful study. Mutual interference and radar returns from unexpected sources were most often the causes. One of the most surprising were the radar return signals from the moon. These were caused by the introduction of more powerful radars. The puzzling part was the delay of several seconds before the return signals showed up on the radar screen. It was finally determined that this was the time it took for the signal to travel all the way to the moon and return.

One interesting example of mutual interference was the case of a Norfolk, VA, radar. The radar operators were picking up a radar blip, indicating a target, but interceptors were unable to find any object in the area. After much testing, it was found that the cause was mutual interference from a radar at Saint John's in Newfoundland. The strangest part was that changing the pulse repetition frequency (PRF) would cause the blip on the screen to move, giving the indication of a moving target. As a radar officer, I could understand the possibility of mutual interference if the atmospheric conditions were correct, but I never did understand how changing the PRF could make the target move on the radar screen.

There were other returns that were classified as "spurious" radar reflections. They were probably caused by unusual atmospheric conditions or strange signals that crept into the electronic components of the radars.

Next: There were actual objects, which were found on the ground. Every object that descended to the earth was carefully examined to determine its origin. All were satisfactorily explained.

Some items did not fall from the sky but had a much closer origin, for example, a neighbor's lawn mower. Almost all objects that fell from the sky had their origin on earth. This was the era before the tremendous amount of space junk that exists today. Some items were from a few errant missiles that were being tested, but most were from airplanes. I never did understand how a toilet seat fell out of an airplane.

Occasionally, there were tiny space particles, such as meteoroids.

Finally: There were visual sightings. These were the most difficult to explain. Some sightings were from highly respected sources, i.e., pilots, educators, etc.. Most often it was from the result of an unknown or unusual atmospheric condition. In many instances, this phenomena resulted from a reflection under strange conditions, or from some unusual source. Since there was no physical evidence to examine, a positive origin could not always be determined. Reliance had to be placed upon the person's veracity, visual capacity, mental state, and/or emotional status.

Countless studies of the incidents showed that there was no positive proof that the sighting of an actual physical object ever took place. Despite the fact that there was no scientific proof to the contrary, NORAD never relaxed its vigilance.

Among us non-scientific types, there was the feeling that most were simply "copycat sightings." Whenever there was a UFO sighting, invariably there were a number of similar sightings reported over the next few days. We could almost hold a lottery on the exact number of copycat sightings that would occur. Some of us felt that there would be fewer sightings of UFO's if the individuals involved used a better quality bourbon.

It was during this period that the US Air Force Academy was established at Colorado Springs. Originally, the Air Corps had been part of the US Army. After World War II, it was established as a separate military service, but its officers were being trained at West Point. There was much lobbying for the Air Force to have its own military academy. Colorado Springs was chosen.

Some thought that the site chosen was strange for an Air Force Academy. It was at the very base of some of the highest mountains in the United States. Its airfield was out in the flats, a number of miles from the academy. Did the successful fishing of President Eisenhower in Colorado have anything to do with the decision?

In the summer of 1957, I was selected to attend the Army Command & General Staff College at Fort Leavenworth, Kansas. Before leaving, I was presented with a Certificate of Achievement. The following photograph is included for two reasons.

1. It was the first Certificate of Achievement that I had ever received.
2. It's a nice picture.

Col. Burnham   Lt. Gen. Mickelsen   Major Genero

CERTIFICATE OF ACHIEVEMENT AWARD
(official US Army Photograph)

CHAPTER 13

US ARMY COMMAND & GENERAL STAFF COLLEGE

Preface:

The Command & General College was located at Fort Leavenworth, KS. The course was one year in duration and trained Army officers to be effective and competent General Staff officers at all higher echelons of command up to and including the Pentagon.

We moved there with our families and lived in converted WW II wooden barracks. It was crowded and not exceedingly comfortable. One excellent feature of the accommodations was that there was a practice golf course across the street from our quarters. I immediately obtained a set of golf clubs. I tried and tried, but alas, never did break 100. On a related subject, our volley ball team did manage to win the class championship.

Our class consisted of approximately 350 officers, about 50 from the other US military services and about another 50 from foreign countries. The course was totally academic in nature, no field trips.

We learned the functions and capabilities of every branch of service in the Army. We were then taught how to combine all of the branches into the most effective force possible. Next, we studied the deployment and operational use of these forces in all possible situations, in all climatic conditions, and in all probable geographic locations.

Great emphasis was placed on the study of countless tactical situations and possible courses of action for each of them. Then, we conducted a comparative analysis of each. Next, we prepared war plans for the course of action, which we thought had the best chance for success. Finally, we had to defend our plan against those prepared by the other study groups.

Our duties were routine in nature and quite tedious. However, there were a couple of situations which took place during the school year, which may be of interest to the reader.

Foreign Officers
Sputnik
Epigram

Foreign Officers:

As noted earlier there were about 50 foreign officers, only one or two per country. They all spoke English, and we all went to the same classes, took the same examinations, and participated in the same athletic events. In fact the star player on our championship volleyball team was an officer from Ethiopia.

There was one interesting exchange in our sub-group between a West German officer and a British officer. During the study of one tactical situation, we could not agree on a solution. There was much discussion concerning each course of action which was proposed. The German officer wanted to mass our forces, select the most favorable terrain, and launch a massive frontal assault against the enemy. The British officer wanted to deceive the enemy for an extended period. There would be false radio transmissions, false intelligence reports, and many "behind the lines" feints and maneuvers. When he thought that the enemy was confused, he would attack over the most unfavorable terrain. After much discussion of both plans, we were still unable to arrive at an agreed course of action.

Finally, the German officer almost exploded. He looked at the British officer and told him that the British did not want "to fight." He said that all they wanted to do was "to fool" the enemy. (Not too erroneous an observation).

As can be expected, there were extremes among the foreign officers. At one end of the spectrum were the two officers from Communist Yugoslavia. This was the era when the US international strategy was to "woo" Yugoslavia away from the Communist block countries in Eastern Europe.

The two officers lived in an austere manner and seldom, if ever, made off base visits. They were pleasant and respectful at all times. It was almost as if they were trying to fade into the woodwork. One evening at the officers club, I noticed that one of them was trying to hide his military cap. The emblem on the cap was a large Communist Red Star. He did want to call attention to the fact that he was from a Communist country.

Evidently, the US strategy worked. Yugoslavia became independent from the Soviet block. However, the aftermath was very sad. The country descended into a prolonged and bloody civil war. It became completely dismembered. What role these two officers played in the disintegration of Yugoslavia is unknown.

At the other end of the spectrum was (Colonel/General ?) Rafael Trujillo, son of the "President-For-Life" of the Dominican Republic. Contrary to the Yugoslavian officers, he lived off base in a lavish life style. He rented a very large villa for his family and entourage (friends, body guards, etc.).

During the first half of the school year, he did reasonably well. He even sponsored a fabulous champagne party for the officers (and wives) who were in his class sub-group. It was in the grand ballroom of the Muehlebach Hotel in Kansas City. For entertainment, the famous Xavier Cugat band was flown from

New York City where they were performing at the Waldorf Astoria Hotel. A grand time was had by all.

However, a dramatic change took place during the second half of the school year. He had sick leave to go to Los Angeles for medical treatment. There he engaged in a life style that was unbelievably extravagant. Rafael partied with the rich, the famous, and the most glamorous stars of Hollywood. The gifts which were dispensed to his favorites were legendary. They were very expensive items of jewelry and even a sports car.

All of this did not escape the attention of the American media. *Time* magazine lead the attack with a scathing lead story about his Hollywood antics. *Time* went on to attack the Army for having permitted the son of a Latin American dictator attend the Command & General College. Ignored was the fact that Rafael's father was an strong anti Communist and an ardent supporter of US foreign policy. The Dominican Republic was the only country in Latin America to open its doors to the Jewish refugees from Europe.

At the end of the course, (Colonel/General ?) Rafael Trujillo was not permitted to graduate with his class. He was called into the Commandant's office and simply given a Certificate of Attendance.

The ending of the Rafael Trujillo story was not unusual for Latin America. His father was assassinated. Rafael took over the reigns of government for a short time. He had the assassins assassinated. Then he went into semi voluntary exile aboard his yacht to the sunny French Rivera.

Sputnick:

Although not involved directly with the Command & General Staff College, an event took place while I was there, which had monumental consequences. It was the successful launching by the Soviet Union on the 4th of October 1957 of Sputnik, the world's first space satellite.

It kept circling the earth, sending out triumphant messages to the entire world. The Soviet Union was proclaiming that it was the world's leader in technological advancement. Overnight, the United States lost its preeminence in the scientific field. It took ten years to regain that supremacy.

President Eisenhower ordered the immediate launching of an American space satellite. It was to be launched by the Vanguard missile, which was built by the Glen L. Martin Aviation Company and funded by the Navy. It was made ready for launch in December. However, to add insult to injury, it exploded into a giant fireball while still on the launching pad.

The President then contacted the Army missile team at the Redstone Arsenal in Huntsville, Alabama. It was commanded by General Medaris. Wernher Von Braun was his chief scientist. They were asked how soon they could launch a satellite into space. They told the president it would take six weeks. Two days less than six weeks, the Army missile team launched the first American satellite into space. I remember a group of us watching the launch on our small TV's. As the rocket was lifting off, it was almost as if everyone was murmuring a silent prayer for its success. Explorer I achieved a successful orbit.

EXPLORER I US ARMY ARSENAL MISSILE TEAM
(seated center General Medaris and Wernher von Braun)

The background to this event is both interesting and a little sad. At that time, the best and most advanced missile scientists and technicians in the world were with the General Medaris/Wernher von Braun team at the Redstone Arsenal. The American aviation industry had virtually no experience in this field. However, they had one asset that was denied to the team in Huntsville. They were highly skilled at "brochuremanship." In other words, the aviation industry spokesmen were highly skilled at selling their product by means of brochures, sketches, drawings (artist conceptions), and models. In addition, they had great support from the media, partly as a result of their enormous advertising budgets. They controlled the "spin" that was published concerning their products in the public media. The American aviation industry was enormous and quite skilled. Given enough time and money it could do almost anything.

The Army team at Redstone was unable to compete with the aviation industry. It had tight budgetary constraints. Because it was a government agency, it was forbidden to advertise the capabilities of its products in the media. The Army team tried to exhibit its capabilities by public demonstrations. However these were sharply curtailed for security reasons. Eighteen months before Sputnik, the Army wanted to launch a space satellite. President Eisenhower forbid the Army from doing so. For some strange reason, he wanted our first satellite to be launched by a civilian company.

The Redstone team realized the importance of being "first in space." It was going to launch the first satellite "by accident." When the White House learned of this, a special representative was sent to Huntsville, forbidding them from doing so. There were even threats of disciplinary action should orders from Washington be ignored. As a result, America was not first in space. It might be mentioned that when President Kennedy took office, he immediately turned to the General Medaris/Wernher von Braun team in order to put a man on the moon within the next ten years.

In so far as written history is concerned, the Soviet Union will be credited with being the first nation to successfully launch a space satellite. As for President Eisenhower, he will probably be remembered most for his final speech. In it, he warned that the nation must beware of "the military-industrial complex."

Epigram:

After graduation from the Command & General College, I was assigned to the Pentagon. En route, our family took a vacation in New York and we visited our relatives. One day, I wandered through our old neighborhood on Manhattan's westside. There was a tavern there owned by a member of our old crowd. Upon entering, Jack the bartender, saw me and in a clear audible voice asked where I had been. They had not seen me in over a year.

I replied in an equally audible voice that I had spent the last year in Leavenworth. Immediately, all drinking and conversation ceased. The place became unearthly quiet and all heads turned to stare at me. It was then that I realized that on the westside of New York, "Leavenworth" did not carry the connotation of the Army Command & General Staff College. There, it meant only one thing: a Federal Penitentiary for hardened criminals.

CHAPTER 14

PENTAGON

Preface:

This chapter concerns my tour of duty at the Pentagon. It was the longest and most important duty assignment of my 26 years of military service. Therefore, this chapter is greater in length and more diverse than any of the other chapters in this volume.

All of the incidents described in this chapter took place while I was assigned to the Army General Staff in the Pentagon. The following is a broad outline of the functions of the Army General Staff at that time. It is being included to aid the reader in understanding my role in the events described.

The most senior military officer in the Department of Defense was the Chairman of the Joint Chiefs of Staff. The Joint Chiefs of Staff was composed of the Chiefs of the four military services (Army, Navy, Air Force, and Marines). The position of Chairman was normally rotated among the four services. The working staff was composed of officers form the four services, their number corresponding to the strength of their respective service.

In the Army, the most senior officer was the Chief of Staff of the US Army. His principal assistants were the four "Deputy" Chiefs of Staff.

Deputy Chief of Staff for Personnel
Deputy Chief of Staff for Intelligence
Deputy Chief of Staff for War plans and Operations
Deputy Chief of Staff for Logistics

The duties and responsibilities of the Deputy Chiefs of Staff for Personnel and Intelligence are self evident.

The office of the Deputy Chief for War Plans and Operations was the "lead" staff agency of the Army. It was responsible for developing plans for every conceivable military operation, in every part of the world. Literally, there were a hundred such contingency plans. In addition, they constantly monitored the activities of all Army units, worldwide. The staff was composed generally of officers from the three combat arms (Infantry, Artillery, and Armor). Assignment to this staff was considered a stepping stone to a bright military future. The most renown graduate from this staff was General, later President, Dwight D. Eisenhower.

The Deputy Chief for Logistics was responsible for insuring that adequate logistics support was provided for all Army plans and operations. In order to carry out his responsibilities, he was given control and supervision over the seven technical support branches:

Engineer
Quartermaster
Signal
Transportation
Chemical
Medical
Ordnance

The Logistics General Staff was composed mostly of officers from the seven technical support branches listed above. The "lead" element of the Logistics General Staff was the Plans Division. All logistics "operational" functions were carried out by the seven technical support branches. In other words, if the

Logistics General Staff had a requirement, they simply passed it on to the appropriate technical support branch. The technical support branches were the ones who actually fulfilled the requirement.

The Plans Division was organized into three planning branches: The European Branch, The Far East Branch, and the Western-Hemisphere Branch. The European Branch, including Africa and the Middle East, was considered the most important branch. Therefore, the most experienced logistics officers were assigned to that branch. The Far East Branch was considered next in importance and was staffed with the next most experienced logistics officers. The remainder of the officers were assigned to the Western Hemisphere Branch.

All miscellaneous activities seemed to fall within the purview of the Western Hemisphere Branch. The author (an Artillery officer) was assigned to this branch. I was the only trained nuclear weapons effects officer in the Plans Division. The Western Hemisphere Branch was responsible for the logistics support of Army troops in such places as Thule (Greenland), Alaska, and the Panama Canal Zone. It was responsible for establishing and maintaining the Army Relocation Site deep in the Appalachian Mountains (to be used in event of a nuclear attack). This branch also participated in War Games within the Army and with the other military services. Later, it became responsible for the logistics support of all Army activities involving Cuba.

Two additional points should be added for further clarification.

(1) Officers on the Army General Staff were considered to be "universal" officers. Their responsibilities to their basic branch (Artillery, Signal, etc.), were subordinated to their duties as a "General Staff" officer. To emphasize this point, they wore a distinctive General Staff insignia and General Staff identification badge, see next page.

GENERAL STAFF INSIGNIA | GENERAL STAFF IDENTIFICATION

(2) General Staff officers were Colonels, Lieutenant Colonels and a few senior Majors. They were commonly referred to as "action officers." They did all of the work. They wrote the plans and memorandums, conducted the studies, and coordinated actions with the other military services and governmental agencies. Once approval was obtained from their senior officers, they issued the appropriate orders and monitored the implementation of those orders. They kept their superiors informed of the results and wrote the "after action" reports. Literally, they were the "foot soldiers" of the Pentagon.

Who would have thought that forty years later, the soft and quiet environment of the Pentagon would be transformed into a "combat zone."

Among my other duties, I was involved in the following six events during my tour in the Pentagon:

> *PAMUSA-60*
> *(Post Attack Mobilization, US Army - 1960)*
> *The Bay of Pigs*
> *Earthquake in Chile*
> *(A disaster Relief Operation That Went Well)*
> *The Berlin Wall*
> *Crisis in Panama*
> *Cuban Missile Crisis*

PAMUSA-60   (Post Attack Mobilization US Army -1960):

Shortly after being assigned to the Logistics General Staff, I was placed on semi-detached service with the PAMUSA-60 study task force. It was engaged in a mammoth war/study to determine if the United States could survive an all-out nuclear war.

The officer in charge of the study was Colonel C. H. Lee, son of General John (Courthouse) Lee of WWI and WWII fame. Engaged in the study were about 125 officers, with all military services participating. Also engaged in the study were about two dozen civilian scientist. They were led by Herman Kahn from the Rand Corporation. His book, <u>On Thermo-nuclear War</u>, was considered to be the most authoritative non-military book on the subject. Later, he went on to become one of the founders of the Hudson Institute, a highly respected and renowned Think Tank.

PAMUSA-60 took over one year to complete, At that time, it was the most thorough and comprehensive study that had ever been conducted on the subject. It used the most advanced and sophisticated computer in the United States. Its data bank contained the exact geographic location of every significant military installation, industrial facility, public utility, transportation infrastructure, population center, etc., in the United States. Of most importance, the study group had access to the best US intelligence estimates of the Soviet war plans and nuclear arsenal. It also had access to the US nuclear arsenal and war plans.

The basic assumption used was that the Soviets would exercise their "first strike" capability and that there would be a massive US retaliation. It was also assumed that there would not have been a massive US pre-attack shelter building program. However, there would have been an intensive educational program on how to make maximum use of whatever public and private shelters were already available. For example, people would be advised to pre-stock their basements and take shelter in them, similar to what happened during the Cuban Missile Crisis.

After the simulated attack, an estimate was made of US casualties and physical damage. Then, it was the responsibility of my team to determine what size Army force could be logistically supported, within national residual capabilities.

Assuming that the results are no longer valid, I believe that I can now summarize the basic findings, without compromising national security. The results were that the United States would suffer severe physical damage and enormous personnel casualties. It would be somewhat similar to, or maybe a little greater than, what the Soviets suffered during WW II. Basically, the study concluded that United States could survive, and within 12 months, organize, equip, train and deploy 25+ Army divisions.

The Soviet Union, despite the enormous physical damage and personnel casualties they suffered during WW II, went on to become one of the super powers of the world. Could we expect anything less from the United States?

At the end of the study, I was assigned the task of writing a memorandum to the President summarizing the results. It was not too difficult a task, since all White House memorandums were limited to one page. I ended the memorandum as follows, "PAMUSA-60 proves conclusively that the United States could survive a nuclear attack, and that we would be neither all red nor all dead."

About two weeks later, President Kennedy gave a speech at Fort Bragg. He told the troops not to fear the Soviet Union, and that even in the event of a nuclear attack, "We would be neither all red nor all dead."

Bay of Pigs:

I was only on the fringes of the Bay of Pigs fiasco. What I learned and what is described in this chapter was derived from a number of sources:

> The Chief of the Western Hemisphere Branch, my boss, was heavily involved.
> Osmosis, since my coworkers were deeply involved.
> Attendance at an "after action" de-briefing given by the CIA officials who had been responsible.
> For over 20 years, I lived and worked in the Miami area with victims and participants in the event.

The plan to organize, equip and train exiled Cubans for their return to Cuba, originated during the Eisenhower administration. Vice President Nixon was a big proponent of the plan. Originally, it was a well kept secret.

This changed during the last half of 1960. During the Nixon/ Kennedy presidential debates, Kennedy publicly announced that if he were president, he would arm exiled Cubans and support their invasion of Cuba. Nixon was stunned. In an effort to maintain its secrecy, he replied that such a plan was neither proper, nor feasible. Despite Nixon's public denial, preparations to implement the plan continued, although it was no longer a closely held secret.

The plan was not complicated. The armed Cuban exiles were to be landed in Eastern Cuba near Trinidad, about 400 kilometers from Havana. Once ashore, the exiles would join the counter-revolutionary forces already operating in the nearby Escambray mountainous area. The timimg was to be during the feast of the Three Kings, shortly after Christmas. It was the most important and celebrated holiday of the year in Cuba. Also, it would be during the "lame duck" period of Eisenhower's presidency, so that he could assume all blame in event of failure.

Together, this combined force would take effective control of a populated area. They would establish a "national redoubt", and declare themselves to be the legitimate government of Cuba. Once established, the US Government would quickly recognize them as the "official" government of Cuba, and begin "overtly" providing massive logistic support. This was to be one of the responsibilities of our Western-Hemisphere Branch.

The Escambray mountains would have created severe operational problems for Castro's tank force. Given "incidental" air cover, semi-naval support, and unlimited logistics support, it would have been only a matter of time before the counter-revolutionary forces prevailed.

After the election in 1960, President-elect Kennedy virtually pleaded with the still-President Eisenhower, not to proceed with the plan. He reasoned that implementation of the plan might complicate and detract from his inauguration. He promised to implement the plan as soon as he was firmly in office. President Eisenhower agreed to his request.

After President Kennedy assumed office, he reviewed the Eisenhower plan in detail. He was very displeased with the plan's slow and gradual approach to the counter-revolution. President Kennedy insisted that the landings take place close to the Capitol. Since there had been reports of wide spread dissatisfaction with Castro, it was assumed that the general population would rise up and support the invaders. In that manner, the invading Cubans could quickly march into Havana and take control of the government.

The Chairman of the Joint Chiefs of Staff and the Director of the CIA vehemently opposed Present Kennedy's changes. They pointed out that the invasion force was too small and too lightly armed to engage the much stronger Castro force. They also pointed out that Castro now had the excellent T-54 Soviet tank, as well as hundreds of Soviet military advisors.

After much debate, and especially since the plan was no longer a tightly held secret, the CIA and the Joint Chiefs accepted President Kennedy's plan, but only on three conditions: (1) that the Cuban Air Force be destroyed before landing, (2) that the invasion force receive air cover during landing, and (3) that close air support be provided after landing. President Kennedy agreed. However the changes caused a delay of about three months. Appropriate planes had to be found (WW II B-25 bombers from the Air National Guard), and put into a combat mode (armed, loaded with bombs, insignia's changed, etc.). Volunteer crews had to be found and trained. All had to be assembled in Central America to give the appearance of non US involvement.

This three month gap was critical. During this period, Castro rounded up, imprisoned and tortured over a hundred thousand potential counter-revolutionary supporters. One of my associates told me how he saw Castro's police take his father and brother, lock them in a storage shed and then set it afire. Both were burned to death.

The new site selected for the landing was an unprotected and vulnerable area called the Bay of Pigs. It was a swampland on the south side of the island, about 80 miles from Havana. It had only very limited access roads to the interior, see map. Since the details of the landing were covered by countless contemporary sources, I will go into those items not well publicized, or perhaps, less well known.

The air attack to destroy Castro's Air Force was to last over a two day period. The air attack began on April 15, 1961. Its origin could not be completely disguised. Initially, US involvement was denied. Ambassador Adlai Stevenson made a statement to that effect in the United Nations on the first day of the attack. By the end of the first day, it became obvious to the world that the air attack had its origins in the United States. Upon learning this, Ambassador Stevenson became enraged. He had publicly made a statement which was obviously not true.

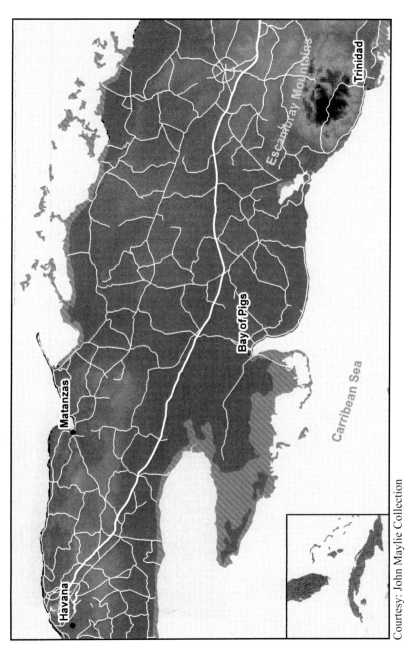

CUBA

Courtesy: John Maylie Collection

177

It must be remembered that at this time, Adlai Stevenson was probably the most beloved and respected liberal politician in the country. He told the President that unless further US sponsored air attacks were cancelled, he would resign his position as the US Ambassador to the United Nations. Then, the whole world would know that he had been deceived.

Washington itself was becoming uneasy at its public denials of US involvement. It was Ambassador Stevenson's strenuous objections that tipped the scales and stopped all further direct US involvement. This was despite the President's previous agreement with the CIA and Joint Chiefs of Staff. President Kennedy's decision to halt further US direct involvement sealed the fate of the invasion force.

As to whether the invasion with adequate air support would have been successful and welcomed by the populous, there were indications that it would have had a high probability of success. One exiled doctor tells the story that upon hearing of the landing, much of the Guardia National started to fall apart. One of the members actually came to the doctor's office and surrendered his rifle. He said that he was only a member of militia because he was forced into it. Later, when they heard of the plight of the landing force, they changed their loyalty back to Castro.

Another item of interest was told by a Navy commander, who was a pilot in the carrier task force which was to support the landing. He told of how their planes were fueled, armed and ready for take off to support the landing, when they were ordered to cease operations. He said that there were almost tears in the eyes of his fellow pilots, because they knew what the outcome of the landing would be.

Although President Kennedy publicly assumed responsibility for the failure of the Bay of Pigs fiasco the average American was left with the impression that the CIA and the military gave the

President poor advice. Allen Dulles, head of the CIA, and his top assistants were asked to resign. General Lemnitzer, Chairman of the Joint Chiefs of Staff, was permitted to complete his two year tour, but was not asked to remain for a second tour, as was customary. According to the Washington spin machine, he was promoted (?) to a subordinate command in Europe.

There was also a technical factor which entered into the equation. For an assault landing, ships are combat loaded, with troops, ammunition, supplies, all together. Since the initial plans did not call for an assault type landing, the ships were loaded in an administrative manner to make maximum use of the limited shipping space available. The ship carrying the ammunition and heavy weapons was sunk. This left the lightly armed landing force with only small arms to defend itself.

Finally, as was pointed out earlier, Castro had a modest tank force, armed with the excellent Soviet T-54, the most widely used tank in the world since WW II. There were also hundreds of Soviet military advisors in Cuba. It was these tanks which lead in the advance against the landing force. These tanks could have been decimated by naval close air support if it had been made available.

In battle, the tank commanders communicate with one another by radio. Radio transmissions are susceptible to intercept. It was strange that language used in these communications, was not Spanish.

Given the above scenario, it can be seen why the Cuban community in Miami is one Latin American group in the United States that is staunchly Republican.

Earthquake in Chile:
(A disaster relief operation that went well)

D - DAY

On Sunday May 21, 1961, a devastating earthquake, measuring 8.6 on the Richter Scale rumbled through central Chile. Initial estimates by the President of Chile were 6,000 - 10,000 people dead or missing; 2,000,000 homeless; and $3,000,000,000 in damages. Later, these figures were revised downward.

It was considered to be the most intense earthquake of the century in the Western Hemisphere. The earthquake was so severe that it caused a Tsunami wave that traveled across the Pacific Ocean. It caused over 60 fatalities in Hawaii and about 200 fatalities in Japan.

The scope of the disaster was so great, that the US Ambassador to Chile got in touch with President Kennedy as soon as it was possible and pleaded for assistance. The President agreed to help and even allocated $6,000,000 from the president's contingency fund to support the effort.

Since the city of Concepcion was in the center of the earthquake area, the US Ambassador requested that our disaster relief efforts be centered in that city.

At that time, there was no single federal agency responsible for planning and conducting large scale disaster relief operations, especially in foreign countries. Further, there were no supplies or equipment set aside or earmarked for that purpose. As a result, President Kennedy turned to the Secretary of Defense, Robert McNamara, for assistance.

Also, it might be mentioned that this was shortly after the Bay of Pigs fiasco, and the President was trying to improve his international reputation.

Early the next morning the Secretary of Defense called a meeting of the Joint Chiefs of Staff, and directed them to prepare a plan for major disaster relief operations in Chile. He established a six hour deadline. The Secretary of Defense who was well known for his fiscal acumen, specified a $6,000,000 cap for the project. While each service, (Navy, Air Force, and Army) was prepared to participate, each had certain advantages and disadvantages.

NAVY: The Navy with the Marines were handicapped in that most of their operational forces were already deployed in distant overseas areas; i.e., Far East and Mediterranean. Use of their domestic resources would take several days to assemble and about two weeks to ship via sea transport to Chile.

AIR FORCE: At that time, the Air Force felt that it was the dominate military service. They were anxious to flex their muscles and prove their point. Since the Air Force did not have appropriate ground units, they committed themselves to providing unlimited air transport support for whatever disaster relief assistance was decided upon.

ARMY: As a result of the above, the Army was directed to develop the overall plan for American disaster relief assistance and to provide whatever ground support elements were deemed appropriate.

Before proceeding there are two points which should be mentioned:

1. Standing Operating Procedures (SOP) in the Army were that the War Plans and Operations Staff, with their combat arms officers (Infantry, Artillery and Armor), would prepare all operational plans. The Logistics Staff, with its officers from the seven technical support branches, would merely insure that the operations received proper logistics support.

2. At that time, the Army had many of its combat units deployed in Europe and the Far East. All units in Continental United States were on a training and maintenance status, except for those units assigned to STRAC (Strategic Army Corps). Units were assigned to STRAC on a rotational basis and kept on a semi-alert status. Leaves were restricted and all initial supplies and equipment, including arms and ammunition, were kept physically on base and ready for instant deployment.

In the topsy-turvy world of the Pentagon, and for reasons known only to the Army Chief of Staff, the responsibility for planning and implementing the entire disaster relief operation was assigned to the Logistics staff. It so happened that in the Western Hemisphere Branch, there was a combat arms officer (myself), and most importantly, I was "available." Naturally, I was assigned the responsibility for planning and implementing the Chilean disaster relief operation.

Upon receiving the assignment, I immediately contacted my counterparts in the seven technical support branches (Quartermaster, Medical, Engineer, Transportation, Signal, Ordnance, and Chemical). Each was asked what their respective branches could contribute and to designate the units to participate. Also, they were asked to recommend the types and quantities of supplies and equipment to accompany the troops. They were given a four hour deadline. Since security was not involved, communications by phone were permitted.

Early in the afternoon, the recommendations of the technical support branches began arriving in the logistics plans office. Here, they were added to, subtracted from, and modified as deemed appropriate. An outline plan was prepared and presented to the Joint Chiefs of Staff and the Secretary of Defense that afternoon. They approved it and hand carried it to the White House before close of business that same day.

The basic components of the plan were to airlift immediately the following support units to Concepcion, Chile:

Two Mobile Field Hospitals (similar to M*A*S*H on television)
Two water purification units
Two mobile laundry units
Two field shower/wash units
Tens of thousands of field rations
Hundreds of tents for shelters
Four Medical Evacuation Helicopters
Local and long distance field communications
Cargo and personnel support vehicles
Security detachments from the combat arms

That evening, President Kennedy approved the plan and ordered its implementation.

D DAY + 2

The Air Force lived up to its commitment. Early the next morning, a great number of air transports began arriving at designated Army bases. With a minimum of delay, loading operations began for the disaster relief troops, supplies, and equipment.

By the end of the day, some of the aircraft were already on their way to Chile. Because of the great distance involved (over 5,000 miles), the planes landed in the Panama Canal Zone for refueling and servicing.

Even before this, the Air Force had already dispatched one of its "Path Finder' units to Chile. The Air Force maintained at least one "Path Finder" unit on constant alert and ready for instant deployment. It was trained to land by parachute, if necessary. The units were equipped with radars, communications equipment, and navigation aids. Once the "path finders" landed, their mission was to secure an air landing site; in this instance, it was the

Concepcion Airport. Then, as soon as possible, they were to establish a complete air traffic control capability. This included not only the landing and taking off of aircraft, but also their parking as well. The latter was to insure that the transport aircraft could be unloaded safely and without local or mutual interference.

D DAY + 3

The massive airlift of personnel, supplies, and equipment continued at an accelerated pace.

The initial disaster relief elements began arriving in Chile late in the afternoon. The first task of these elements was to find suitable locations for the hospitals and supporting facilities. Once located, their next task was to secure the areas selected.

By the end of the day, most of the advance echelons of the units involved had arrived. They proceeded to the sites selected and began to set up the field hospitals, supply depots, etc.

There was much destruction and debris in the area. However, it was the overall emotional atmosphere and the feeling of helplessness and hopelessness exhibited by the local population that was the most saddening. The people seemed to be in a state of shock, meandering aimlessly all over the area. In general terms, they appeared to be in some form of a daze.

There was no significant or organized form of local leadership. Routine governmental activities appeared to be non-existent. Search and rescue operations were conducted on a personal and individual basis.

In other words, the population of Concepcion needed not only material aid, but a boost in morale as well.

The massive airlift continued and the arrival of personnel, supplies and equipment peaked.

The two field hospitals and their supporting elements, such as the water purification and laundry units, continued to be set up. The supplies of rations, tents, and folding cots were being gathered, stacked and stored in controlled environments. The erection of the tent cities to shelter the homeless was begun. The rotor blades of the medical evacuation helicopters were being re-attached and the helicopters were put into service. Local and long distance communications were becoming operational. All was being made ready for conducting full scale disaster relief operations the next day.

However, the most dramatic change that took place on DAYS 3 & 4, was in the morale and spirit of the local population. Once the people saw the magnitude of the airlift, with all of the personnel, supplies and equipment, they realized that they were no longer alone, and that their situation was not hopeless. They began to act with determination and self reliance, not only helping themselves, but one another as well. They were even beginning to smile again.

Many of them gathered around the two field hospitals, and within their capabilities, offered their services. They helped to erect the tent cities, move and stack supplies, and, yes, even dig latrines. Of course, they received a little incentive with an extra issue of food rations.

Almost equally as important, local officials began appearing on the scene. They centered their activities near the two field hospitals. They began to assemble their staffs and work crews. They organized search and rescue operations. Their two top priorities were restoring utilities and public services. Clearing thoroughfares and the removal of debris were to come later.

Of course there were glitches, but on the whole, things proceeded quite smoothly. For the indigenous population, the outlook for the future brightened immeasurably. The whole area was permeated with a new "can do" attitude.

D DAY +5

This was the day all disaster relief efforts began operating at full capacity.

The field hospitals received swarms of patients, but fortunately, they were not overwhelmed. The military detachments, along with some local security personnel, maintained a fair semblance of order. Also, the field hospital staffs were augumented by local medical personnel whose hospitals were severely damaged or had run out of medical supplies.

All proceeded in a relative orderly manner, and there were no reports of serious mishaps, or maltreatments. It was not long before the field hospital spaces became crowded and treatments were being conducted on an "out-patient" basis.

The great demands for food and shelter were being alleviated with the distribution of emergency food rations and the availability of living quarters in the tent cities. As with the field hospitals, order was maintained by the US Army detachments and some local volunteers.

As may be surmised, the water purification units were immediately overwhelmed. Lines of local inhabitants arrived with all sorts of water carrying containers. A pleasant surprise was the great popularity of the shower/washing facilities. The laundry units also operated at maximum capability to meet both US and local medical needs.

It was at this time that local governmental agencies began

operating in a semi-effective manner. Their primary focus was still on their search and rescue efforts. However, serious attempts were being made to restore law and order and to re-establish public utilities.

The US disaster relief operations were fortunate in that they could exercise effective command and control by means of their newly established communications system. This was augmented by the use of military vehicles and helicopters.

D DAY + 6, ++++++

After the first few hectic days, things settled down and became more organized and orderly.

The flow of patients became more manageable, and the character of the patients began to change. Patients with injuries directly attributed to the earthquake became fewer, and most of the patient's needs were only indirectly related to the earthquake, i.e. dysentery, etc. There was rumor that even a baby was born in one of the hospitals. Local medical personnel began returning to their indigenous facilities. By the end of the second week, the lines to the field hospital more resembled a "sick call" line at an Army base than an emergency help station for victims of an earthquake.

All of the other supporting elements, water purification, distribution of food, etc. also began to operate in a more organized and effective manner. The laundry and shower/wash facilities continued to operate at maximum capacity. The former helped considerable in meeting the needs of local medical facilities.

By the end of the first week, local government agencies had returned to their former areas or some other suitable location. Search and rescue operations were coming to an end. Governmental units were busy with debris removal, restoration of public utilities, and the opening of main routes of thoroughfare.

About the third week, it became a general feeling among the disaster relief units that the emergency phase was over, and that it was time to return to the United States. The US Ambassador and Chilean officials concurred. However, their approval was based upon one very important contingency. It was based on the premise that only the American personnel would return to the United States. All food, supplies, and equipment would remain in Chile and would be turned over to appropriate Chilean authorities. Helicopters and sensitive communications equipment were the exceptions.

The President, Secretary of Defense and the Joint Chiefs of Staff agreed wholeheartedly. The Air Force was happy that they were relieved of having to conduct a massive retrograde airlift operation. The Army liked the idea because now, they could purchase new equipment for their hospitals since most of the existing medical equipment was of Korean War vintage.

The entire cost of the operation far exceeded the $6,000,000 allocated. However, the disaster relief operation was so successful, from both humanitarian and public relations viewpoints, that funds were found to overcome the deficit.

Later, President Kennedy visited Latin America and was greeted with loud applause, some of which can be attributed to this highly successful disaster relief operation.

LESSONS LEARNED

1. Establish a physical and identifiable presence as soon us humanly possible. It could be a military person in uniform or a civilian with an official looking armband or brassard.

2. Immediately upon arrival, engage in some visible and help-ful activity. It can be as sensitive as establishing pockets of

secure areas or as mundane as directing traffic at a busy intersection.

3. Start providing medical service, water, food, and shelter, as soon as feasible.

4. Leave search and rescue efforts in the hands of local authorities. Assist, if required, with non-available support items, such as helicopters. (Currently, people sniffing dogs are popular.)

5. Leave debris removal and reconstruction in the hands of local authorities. Support with funding, as appropriate.

6. Do not over-stay your presence. Try to leave as soon as the emergency phase is over.

7. When leaving, transfer medical facilities, supplies, and equipment to the local authorities, or appropriate non-governmental organizations.

8. Act promptly, decisively and, if necessary, bend a few rules. During this operation, an Air Force Base in Texas would not move Army troops without a fiscal appropriations number. The desk officer in the Pentagon found an ancient set of personal travel orders, which contained an expired fiscal appropriations number. He read these numbers over the phone to the officials in Texas, and they immediately moved the troops as requested.

The Berlin Wall:

(Historical Background)

As World War II was coming to an end in Europe in 1945, the Western Allied (US, British, and French) Armies, were marching across Germany from the West, and the Soviet Union Armies were advancing from the East. General Patton, Commander of the US Third Army, was planning to march on to Berlin. However, General Eisenhower, the overall Allied Commander, ordered all Allied troops to halt their advance at the Elbe River. The river constituted a natural barrier, going from north to south through the center of Germany. This would prevent the Allied troops from being entangled with the Soviet troops, with possible serious consequences. From a military view point, it was a wise decision.

From a political view point, the decision to halt the Allied advance at the Elbe River was a disaster.

The United States, Great Britain, France, and the Soviet Union had agreed to divide the vanquished Germany into four Occupation Zones. The three Western Allied nations were assigned all of Germany west of the Elbe River, and the Soviets were given control of all Germany east of the Elbe River. The one exception was Berlin. Although located in the center of the Soviet zone, it was established as a separate entity under the joint control of the Western Allies and the Soviet Union.

In 1947 and 1948, the Cold War was just beginning. On June 24, 1948, the Soviets decided to close all land routes of communications between Berlin and the Allied Occupation Zones west of the Elbe River. They believed that by starving out the two million Germans in the Allied Sectors of Berlin, the Allies would be forced to evacuate. This would leave the Soviets in complete control of all of Berlin.

President Truman had other ideas. He ordered the immediate reinforcement of the US garrison in Berlin with a brigade of Army troops. Next, he ordered the most massive airlift in history to provide food and fuel to the Germans in West Berlin. The airlift lasted 321 days, and at its peak, a plane was landing in Berlin with supplies every minute (about 1,400 landings in a 24 hour period). Life in the Allied sectors of Berlin was sustained.

Probably of equal importance was that on the world stage, the Soviet Union became a villain and the United States, Great Britain, and France became heroes. The Soviets suffered such a diplomatic defeat that on May 11, 1949, they ended the blockade.

In the meantime, an impenetrable "Iron Curtain" (Winston Churchill's words) descended from north to south across Europe. It consisted of barbed wire fencing, fortifications, watchtowers, and armed guards. In effect, all Soviet controlled nations of Eastern Europe were sealed off from the independent nations of Western Europe. The irony of the situation was that there was a "hole" in that curtain, i.e., Berlin. The Soviets decided that this "hole" had to be closed. However, it was not until 1961 that a plan was devised to accomplish that objective.

A solution to the problem was offered by Walter Ulbricht and Erich Honecker, the leaders of Soviet occupied East Germany. It was approved by Nikita Khruschev, Premier of the Soviet Union. The solution involved the building of the Berlin Wall, which was about 12 feet high and 60 miles long. Construction began on August 13, 1961. The wall encircled the Western occupied sectors of Berlin. It was constructed of concrete and included barbed wire barriers on the top, front, and back. No one was permitted to pass through the wall without specific permission of the armed security guards. At that time, there were about 60,000 East Germans who commuted daily to work in West Berlin.

The stated purpose of the wall was that it would serve as an "Anti-Fascist Protective Rampart." Its real purpose was to prevent the defection of East Germans (especially the best and the brightest) to West Germany. The week before construction began, almost 2,000 East Germans defected to West Germany.

United States Response To The Berlin Wall:

It seems that after consulting with our allies, it was generally agreed that the United States should take the lead in preparing an appropriate response to the building of the wall. Our Secretary of State, Dean Rusk, announced that the building of the wall was a flagrant violation of the East/West agreement concerning the post war control of Berlin. Further, he stated that he would send a "Vigorous protest to the Soviet Union."

Since the protest had no effect on East Germany or the Soviet Union, President Kennedy sought the advice and assistance of the Secretary of Defense, Robert McNamaara. He, in turn, went to his logistics staff for a solution.

During this period, the Pentagon was a veritable beehive of activity. About 15,000 military personnel and civilian employees were busy in their offices working at their assigned tasks. The corridors were filled with "action officers" scurrying back and forth, insuring that their actions were properly coordinated and processed. Even the corner snack shops were filled with individuals getting a little pick-me-up, so they could more effectively carry out their duties.

At night, the scene was changed dramatically. The lights in the offices were turned off as the personnel departed for home. The snack shops were closed, The miles of corridors were dimly lit an devoid of activity. An eerie silence prevailed throughout the entire building. It was in just such an atmosphere that I began one of the most intense periods of my military service.

At the time, I was attending after-duty night classes in the Pentagon given by the University of Maryland. Late one evening after class, I stopped by my office to pick up some items before going home. I turned on the lights of my office and began gathering my belongings. Suddenly the office door burst open and in rushed the senior logistics duty officer. He explained that he saw the light in the office and was thankful that there was at least one logistics plans officer still in the building. I was then directed to prepare a plan for an appropriate US response to the building of the Berlin Wall. The deadline for the Secretary of Defense was 10:00 AM the following morning.

Because of time restraints, I was unable to consult with my counterparts in other staff agencies. Therefore, responsibility for developing the entire plan rested solely on my shoulders. Besides preparing the plan, I prepared the accompanying slides and graphics. This had the side effect that as a chart/slide flipper and back-up staff officer, I was authorized to attend all subsequent briefings concerning the plan.

Being a western-hemisphere plans officer, I was familiar with the war-time mission of the major combat units located in the Continental United States. In event of hostilities with the Soviet Union, the highest priority would be given to the deployment to Europe, via airlift, of the 101st Airborne Division. They were the famed defenders of Bastone, during the Battle of the Bulge in World War II.

The outline of the plan, which I prepared, called for the Secretary of Defense to order the immediate airlift of the 101st Airborne Division to Europe. The Secretary of Defense would call it a "Training Exercise," not a permanent deployment. It was reasoned that the Army would like the idea since it would be a test to see if the 101st Airborne Division could perform its war-time mission. It was also anticipated that the Air Force would concur since it would be an excellent test of the capabilities of their Air Transportation Command.

The second major element of the plan was a little more devious. It called for a "not too secret" alerting of the 2nd Armored Division at Fort Hood, Texas, for immediate deployment to Europe. Troops on leave would be ordered back to base. Equipment would be brought to full operational status. Supplies would be assembled, packed, crated, and readied for shipment. However, movement orders would be held in abeyance, pending evaluation of the response from East Germany and the Soviet Union, concerning the airlift of the 101st Airborne Division to Europe. It was anticipated that these actions would get their attention, and that they might delay the building of the Berlin Wall. The Allies then could negotiate from a position of strength.

At dawn, after working all night and a quick shower and shave, I presented the outline plan to the Chief of the Logistics Plans Division. He approved the plan and took the lead in presenting the plan to the higher military echelons. At 9:00 AM, the plan was presented to the Army Chief of Staff, who also approved it.

At 10:00 AM, the plan was presented to the Joint Chiefs of Staff, along with the plans presented by the other military services. The Navy indicated that they could add one or two ships to their North Atlantic and Mediterranean fleets. The Air Force stated that they could make a squadron of fighter planes available from their Tactical Air Command. Any more significant response would have to come from the Army.

The Army plan was presented to the Joint Chiefs, and they all thought that it was a good plan. HOWEVER, Secretary of Defense, Robert McNamara strongly disagreed. In terse terms he said that the Army plan was totally unacceptable. His exact words were that implementing the Army plan would lead to "uncontrolled escalation." He directed the Army to come up with a new plan.

Responsibility for preparing a new plan was transferred from the Logistics Staff to the War Plans/Operations Staff. It took about 10 days for them to come up with a plan that was acceptable to the Secretary of Defense. When it was finally approved, it presented a "soft" approach, to the situation. Its main features were that the Army would quietly deploy to Europe a couple of small Signal and Ordinance maintenance detachments, an Engineer unit, and four Transportation Corps Truck Companies.

The Secretary of Defense reasoned that the deployment of these units would improve the readiness of the troops in Europe, while not overly exciting the Soviet Union. As can be expected, the Soviet Union and the East Germans did not become excited, nor were they impressed. They simply continued building the wall.

I returned to my Western Hemisphere logistics duties, where Castro was becoming a major problem.

Two historical footnotes concerning the Berlin Wall:

On June 26, 1963, President Kennedy visited Berlin. He gave a speech to a rousing Berlin crowd. In it, he uttered that famous phrase, "ICH BIN EIN BERLINER". It meant, "I am a Berliner." It received a tumultuous response from the people. (The wall remained an effective barrier for another 26 years).

On June 12, 1987, President Regan visited Berlin and gave a speech. He said, "Mr. Gorbachev, Open this gate. Tear down this wall." (Two years later, the gate was opened and the wall was torn down.) Within three years, West and East Germany were reunited.

Courtesy: Genero Family Collection

BERLIN WALL TODAY
(Much of the wall was broken up into small pieces and sold as souvenirs.)

Crisis In Panama:

There was one incident, which although not momentous in itself, was interesting, at least to me. It took place on Saturday, December 1, 1961.

I was the Army Logistics Duty Officer that day. The Duty Officer from the War Plans and Operations Staff, was a very talented "action officer," who will be called Colonel Ike. This was also the day of the annual Army-Navy football game. It seems that all of the senior Generals and Admirals were either at the game, or at a social gathering watching the game. The Army General who was most available for duty in the Pentagon, was a much decorated combat leader and field commander. However, the Pentagon was not his forte. For purposes of this paper, we call him General Joe.

In the morning, there were reports of a major disturbance brewing in Panama. The General and all of the duty officers assembled in the Army War Room.

BACKGROUND: In 1903, The United States and Panama signed a treaty granting the United States "sovereignty" over a ten mile wide strip of land across Panama in which to build a canal. It was called the Panama Canal Zone, and it was granted in perpetuity, i.e. forever.

In 1956, Egypt nationalized the Suez Canal. This stimulated Panamamians to intensify their claims of "sovereignty" over the Panama Canal Zone. In 1956, the United States granted Panama the right to fly one flag in one specified location in the Canal Zone. This did not satisfy the Panamanians. The demonstrations and riots, some deadly, continued. In 1969, the United States returned the Canal Zone, including the canal, to Panama.

On this Saturday in December, 1961, Panamanians were assembling for one of their demonstrations against United States "sovereignty." Since security of the Canal Zone was an Army responsibility, reports of the situation were fed directly into the Army War Room.

On the morning of December 1st, there were reports of a large number of potential demonstrators gathering in Panama City. One report listed 26 bus-loads of demonstrators headed to Panama City. About an hour later, a report stated that 25 bus-loads of demonstrators had arrived in Panama City. At this report, General Joe sprang into action. He ordered Colonel Ike to immediately dispatch a message to the Commanding General of Canal Zone to find that "missing bus."

Colonel Ike and I looked at each other and quietly shook our heads. Here was the General in Panama trying to cope with a potential serious international incident, and here was General Joe, in the Pentagon, demanding that he find that missing bus, which in all probability, was the result of a simple miscount .

The procedure for dispatching a message from the War Room to the field, was that the action officer (Colonel Ike in this instance) would write/scribble the message on a paper tablet. It was then given to a typist, who put in a proper and readable form. When completed, it was given to the General for modification and /or approval. After final approval, it was hand carried next door to the communications center. There it was encoded and sent via TELEX to the intended recipient.

Colonel Ike slowly and laboriously prepared the message. It then took an inordinate length of time to get it to the General for approval. Finally, it took another inordinate length of time for the message to find its way next door to the communications center.

In the meantime, the demonstrators were gathering in Panama City. Once assembled, they began their march to the Canal Zone "check point." It was protected with strong wire fencing and a heavy presence of US Army troops. The demonstrators demanded entrance to the Canal Zone so that they could raise another Panamanian flag. Entrance was refused. The demonstrators began throwing rocks at the troops who were guarding the check point.

When reports of this reached the Army War room, General Joe, again sprang into action. In a loud commanding voice, he demanded to know how big the rocks were that were being thrown at the American troops. He ordered that another message to be sent to the General in Panama.

Again Colonel Ike and I shook our heads. As before, here was the General in Panama entangled in a sensitive international incident and the Pentagon wanted someone to go out and measure "rocks." The question as to whether "rocks" fell within the purview of logistics was never resolved.

The processing of this message seemed to take even a more inordinate length of time than the message about the missing bus. Also, there appeared to be some delay in the encoding and transmission of the message, whether purposely or not is open to question.

At this point, the tense situation in Panama was relieved not because of any action of our military, but with help from "above." Just as the situation was becoming serious, a tremendous tropical storm burst upon Panama City. The storm was so intense, that the demonstrators decided to repair to the nearest bistro and wait-out the storm. The storm lasted so long, that after a few rum and cokes, the demonstrators decided to go home.

As soon as things in Panama quieted down, Colonel Ike and I returned to our normal duty stations. Neither one of us was interested as to what, if any, were the replies from Panama.

Later Colonel Ike and I mused that if we were on the Soviet General Staff, and had to prepare a plan for a surprise attack on the United States, we would select the day of the Army-Navy football game.

Cuban Missile Crisis:

Early in 1962, I was assigned as the "action officer" for the logistics support for any plan involving the US Army and Cuba. I was the only officer on the Logistics General Staff who had access to all plans for the invasion of Cuba. The basic plan was enormous in size. On legal size paper, it was about the thickness of two telephone books. The plan was classified TOP SECRET, "Eyes Only." No other "action officer" on the Logistics General Staff could have access to the plan without my permission.

All communications concerning the plan were transmitted orally, by person to person contact. Nothing was to be put in writing. The TELEX and telephone were not to be used. I was directed not to discuss the plan with any of my coworkers. The reason for the utmost secrecy was that the White House had just made a public statement to the effect that the United States had no plans for the invasion of Cuba.

On Monday, April 9,1962, I was called into the office of my counterpart on the Joint Staff of the Defense Department. I was told to drop all other activities and to give priority to the plan for the invasion of Cuba. I was given a deadline of 45 days to insure that that all logistic support requirements were completed and ready for instant implementation.

Upon returning to my office, I called a meeting of all of my counterparts in the seven technical support services. I passed on the instructions that I had received from the Joint Staff. Each was assigned responsibility for that part of the plan pertaining to his respective technical service. They were also given a 45 day deadline.

Before proceeding, it is considered appropriate to review the enormous work load that had to be performed by each of the technical services to provide logistics support for the Cuban plan. They had to know the specific units and the exact equipment with which these units were equipped. Because of budgetary restrains, there was only limited "uniformity" in the supplies and equipment even when used by similar units. They did not have the same arms, communications equipment, nor even the same make and model motor vehicles. Also, the requirements for such common items as food and shelter varied from unit to unit. In addition, the exact deployment schedule and transportation requirements had to be calculated into the equation.

All of the requirements for each technical service had to be determined and manually placed onto IBM work sheets. These were then punched onto IBM punch cards. When completed, each technical service would have stacks of thousands of punch cards. If the order was given to implement the plan, each technical support service would simply feed the punch cards into a computer. The supplies and equipment would then flow, on schedule, to their designated locations.

As mentioned previously, the Army had about 100 such contingency plans. Those plans were constantly being changed and up-dated. Each change required considerable time and effort to update their respective logistics support requirements. There was a constant backlog of such work.

By the end of the second day, most of my counterparts reported back that they could not meet the 45 day deadline. On a routine basis, it would take about 90 days. To meet the 45 day deadline, the Secretary of Defense would have to designate the Cuban plan "Top Priority."

As a result, I requested a "secret and non-recorded" meeting with Lieutenant General Colglazier, the Army Deputy Chief Of Staff for Logistics. I explained that in order to meet the 45 day deadline, the Secretary of Defense would have to designate the Cuban plan "Top Priority." General Colglazier told me to sit in his office until his return. The General returned about 45 minutes later. I was not informed of his destination.

General Colglazier told me that a 90 day preparation phase was acceptable. It was important that no undue attention was to be placed on the Cuban plan, and it was to be handled on a routine "need to know" basis. Under no circumstance was word to be leaked out that the United States was actively preparing a plan for an invasion of Cuba.

The logistic requirements for the plan were completed within 90 days.

It turned out that the logistic requirements for the plan were highly complex. One of the limiting factors was transportation. When the President was informed as to how long it would take to "gear-up" for the invasion of Cuba, he was visibly upset. He asked the Joint Staff, "Why can't I order an invasion of Cuba today, and tomorrow have paratroopers rain down all over Cuba?" He was informed that there were not enough paratroop assault aircraft on active duty to accomplish the task. Twenty-six squadrons of Air National Guard troop carrying airplanes would have to be called to active duty, pre-positioned, combat equipped, etc.. At that time, the assault aircraft involved was the C-82 flying boxcar. It had a limited flying range and only a modest troop carrying capacity.

No further mention of the specifics of the plan will be mentioned since some of the basics may still be pertinent. The foregoing is common knowledge since on the 26th of October 1962, President Kennedy ordered the federalization of 26 Air National Guard Squadrons of troop carring planes.

I was surprised to read in the *Washington Post*, that on the 31st of August, Senator Keating asked on the Senate floor what the

President was doing about the IRBMs (Intermediate Range Ballistic Missiles) in Cuba. The Washington "spin machine" went into effect, and the nation was left with the impression that there were no IRBM missiles in Cuba. However, the President immediately launched an investigation to try and find out who leaked the information to Senator Keating.

About that time, I left the Pentagon and was assigned to the Joint Armed Forces Staff College in Norfolk. Most of the remainder was learned through official White House press releases, and highly classified "after action de-briefings" which I attended.

On the 22d of October, President Kennedy made the dramatic announcement to the nation that there were Soviet IRBM missiles in Cuba. A U-2 spy plane had flown over Cuba on October 14 and had taken pictures of them. He put all armed forces on "alert" and ordered a naval blockade of Cuba. He told Premier Khrushchev to withdraw the IRBM missiles from Cuba.

A period of intense negotiations began. On October 26th, there appeared to be a breakthrough in the negotiations. This was the day that the President called 26 Air National Guard troop carrier squadrons to active duty. Full agreement with the Soviet Union was reached on the 28th of October.

The popular conception is that "Kennedy and Khrushchev met "eyeball to eyeball" and that Khrushchev "blinked." Basically this was true, except that Kennedy "blinked" twice. The agreement could be summarized as follows:

Khrushchev agreed to remove all IRBM missiles from Cuba.

Kennedy agreed to the following:
   (1) To leave Castro in power and never invade Cuba.
   (2) To remove all US IRBM missiles from Turkey, and the
       rest of Europe.

At that time, in addition to all of our operational IRBM missile sites in Turkey, the US was constructing 28 additional missile sites in six other European countries. Literally, these sites would have encircled Eastern Russia and their satellites. Among the "action officers" in the Pentagon, there was a common feeling that the US had sold its soul to get permission to install our IRBM missiles in these countries.

Why did the Soviet Union install IRBM missiles in Cuba?

Earlier in the year, Premier Khrushchev invited US Ambassador George Ball to his retreat in the Crimea The Premier pointed across the Black Sea to Turkey. He demanded that US remove its IRBM missiles as they were threatening the Soviet Union. His comments were ignored by the US. It was after this incident, that Premier Khrushchev decided that if the US could threaten the Soviet Union with missiles, he too could threaten the United States with missiles in Cuba.

Given the above scenario, it is small wonder that Premier Khrushchev claimed that the Cuban Missile Crisis was a victory for the Soviet Union. It might also be mentioned that a very senior US General publicly stated that he also thought that the Cuban Missile Crisis was a defeat for the United States.

In retrospect, it was strange that:

> US Intelligence was aware of the Cuban missiles on April 9th.
> Senator Keating knew there were Soviet missiles in Cuba on August 31st.
> However, the President did not know of it until October 14th (?)

To some circles in Washington, it appeared that US reactions to the Cuban Missile Crisis were carefully orchestrated to create an

"October Surprise." It was just before the coming November Congressional elections. At that time President Kennedy's popularity was declining, and there was a possibility that the President's party might lose its control of Congress in the coming November elections. The "October Surprise" had the desired effect. The Nation rallied around and supported the President. The President's party lost only two seats in the House of Representatives.

CHAPTER 15

SECRETARY OF DEFENSE - ROBERT MCNAMARA

I don't believe that VOLUME I would be complete without comments about Secretary of Defense, Robert McNamara. With the exception of President Kennedy, he was the most imposing person of that era.

When he took office, the Department of Defense was only about a dozen years old, and it still operated as a semi-splintered organization. Robert McNamara changed that.

When he became Secretary of Defense, he brought with him a couple of dozen young Ph.D,'s. He assigned them to various key positions throughout the Department. They were commonly referred to as "Whiz Kids" (a popular TV show at that time). Together, they brought order, direction, and common sense to the management of the military services. The following are a few examples:

Secretary McNamara instituted a uniform planning, programming, and budgeting system for all of the military services.

Each service had maintained a different level of War Reserves to tide them over till American industry could be converted to meet their military requirements. The Army's level was 6 months. The Air Force's level was zero (the war would be over in two days). The Navy was someplace in between. He made them all the same, so they could all fight the same war.

Secretary McNamara cancelled the Air Force's BOMARC/SAGE air defense system. It was the most expensive system under development and would be of only limited use in a wartime environment. This was despite the most intense lobbying effort by the aviation industry and certain members of Congress. Secretary McNamara was immune to their colorful brochures and extravagant claims. The SAGE component of the system was turned over to the Federal Transportation Authority, and it became the basis for our air traffic control system. The BOMARC Missile portion of the program was terminated because of its limited effectiveness.

Secretary of Defense McNamara also derailed a proposed "massive" air raid shelter construction program. Instead, he and his staff emphasized a reasonable two pronged alternative. First there would be a national survey to locate and identify with suitable signs and symbols, existing potential shelters. Some would even be pre-stocked with survival supplies and equipment. Next, he would institute an extensive national self help program for the general population. See attached excerpts of Department of Defense directives. Such shelters would not be effective if within the immediate vicinity of the fireball. Depending on the size of the bomb and the altitude of the detonation, the shelters would provide excellent protection from resultant shock waves, fire storms and especially radioactive fallout.

In so far as warfare is concerned, it seemed that Secretary McNamara was a neophyte. Apparently, he did not understand some of the basic principles of warfare such as:

The purpose of warfare is to impose your will upon the enemy.
The incremental or piecemeal commitment of forces is an invitation to disaster.
And, as General MacArthur stated so succinctly, "There is no substitute for Victory."

It appeared that Secretary McNamara considered warfare akin to negotiating a new labor union contract.

Appendix 2
(Annex 10-National Shelter Plan)

Fallout Shelter Surveys:

GUIDE FOR
ARCHITECTS AND ENGINEERS

HP-10-2
National Plan Appendix Series

Executive Office of the President

/IL AND DEFENSE MOBILIZATION

HABITABILITY

Although a potential shelter area may provide excellent shielding from fallout radiation, its worth as a shelter is limited if it is poorly ventilated, deficient in sanitary facilities, or too small for the member of occupants. (See fig. 7.)

The term "capacity," as used in shelter surveys, refers to the number of persons that can be accommodated in a shelter.

At least 12 square feet per person is recommended as a basis for determining capacity of a well-ventilated potential shelter area. The best plan of action during the first 24 hours-which is the critical period for fallout-may be to crowd people into somewhat less space to protect them from the high levels of outside radiation. After

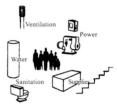

Figure 7.- Shelter Habitability

Department of Defense Fall Out Shelter Directives

DEPARTMENT OF DEFENSE · OFFICE OF CIVIL DEFENSE

FAMILY
SHELTER
DESIGNS

H-7

GENERAL INFORMATION

This shelter is designed to provide low-cost protection from the effects of radioactive fallout. It is intended to be installed below grade in a basement area. Its principal advantages are availability of low-cost materials, adaptability to the dimensions of most basements, ease if construction, and it can be disassembled readily.

TECHNICAL SUMMARY

Space and Occupancy, - The lean-to-shelter interior has over 40 square feet of area and over 120 cubic feet of space and will house three persons. Its length may be extended by adding sections.
Availability and Cost of Materials.- Materials may be purchased from building materials retailers. Many of these have this shelter in kit.

208

CHAPTER 16

FOURTH "ENCOUNTER"

Before closing this volume, I would like to relate my fourth awkward "encounter" involving military aviation. The incident took place before I left the Pentagon.

During my tour of duty in Washington, there was intense rivalry among the military services for the limited amount of funds available in the defense appropriations budget. The two principal protagonists were the Air Force and the Navy.

The Air Force questioned the usefulness of Navy aircraft carriers in actual warfare. The Air Force contended that aircraft carriers were highly vulnerable to air attack and of only limited use. They argued that the funds being wasted on these vulnerable ships should instead, be given to the Air Force to increase the capabilities of their strategic and tactical air arms.

The Navy strongly disagreed They argued that the aircraft carriers were not as vulnerable as the Air Force claimed. Further, the Navy argued that aircraft carriers were essential elements needed to properly defend our nation.

Secretary of Defense, Robert McNamara, and his Whiz Kids decided to conduct a test to determine the validity of the Air Force claims. The Navy was directed to assemble an aircraft carrier task force about 500 to 1,000 miles off the Carolina coast. He then told the Air Force to conduct simulated air attacks against the carrier task force.

For some unknown reason, I was selected to be one of the official Army "neutral" observers for the exercise. We were there to help insure the validity of the results.

Because of my assignment, I was given free access to all parts of the aircraft carrier, including the carrier's Operation's Center, or War Room. For several days, the Air Force conducted simulated attacks, at all altitudes, from all directions, during all weather conditions and at all times, night and day. All their attacks were successfully detected and intercepted.

From the bridge of the carrier, I was able to observe the Navy interceptors taking off and landing at all times of day and night, in all types of weather, and even under "blackout" conditions. All missions were successfully accomplished without a single mishap.

I became firmly convinced that our Navy carrier aircraft pilots were the finest pilots in the world, bar none. In the nearly half century since, I have not seen or heard of anything which would cause me to change my opinion.

It is a matter of record that the Navy aircraft carrier construction program continued as planned.

The reader may question how the preceding constituted my fourth awkward "encounter" with military aviation. Well, the incident happened during our flight out to the aircraft carrier.

Our group of neutral observers boarded a Grumman S2F antisubmarine airplane at the Norfolk Naval Air Station. Since the plane was so reliable, the Navy converted a number of them into passenger and cargo carriers. It had two engines and could land on a carrier was well as on land. The modified plane could accommodate 9 passengers. It was used mostly to carry VIP's, mail, and critical items of supply.

When we tried to land on the deck of the carrier, we were "waved off" at the last instant. We were ordered not to land on the aircraft carrier, but to proceed to the nearest airfield on land. It seems that a warning light came on in the cockpit indicating that the nose wheel would not lock in the "down" position. The ship's Captain did not want to risk a plane crash on the deck of his carrier, so we were ordered back to land.

The pilot of the plane did not believe that we had enough fuel to reach land. As a result we practiced "ditching" procedures repeatedly, and with great attention to detail. However, with the aid of a favorable tail wind, and a few rosaries, we reached land. The nearest airfield was at the Marine Training Base, Cherry Point, North Carolina.

The pilot could not risk a normal landing of our plane, even on land. It could result in the plane tumbling, or even cart wheeling. He improvised a modified landing procedure. The plane approached the airstrip with as little air speed as possible. He touched down at the extreme end of the runway with the plane in a "nose up", "tail down" attitude. The instant the wheels touched down, all passengers and crew members (except the pilot), rushed to the rear of the cabin. We squeezed against the rear bulkhead as tightly as possible. The purpose was to keep the nose wheel in the air and the tail wheel on the ground .

This was one instance when my speed and agility was not a blessing. I was one of the first to hit the bulkhead and one of the most "squeezed" persons on the plane.

Escorted by the crash/rescue teams, the plane coasted to a stop with the nose wheel still not touching the ground. The rescue teams quickly secured the nose wheel. We were then permitted to exit the plane and breathe normally again.

The situation was corrected and the plane was refueled. We took off and landed on the carrier's deck later that afternoon without further incident.

CHAPTER 17

TRANSITION

This appears to be an appropriate time to have Volume I come to an end.

From the Pentagon, I was assigned to the Armed Forces Staff College at the Norfolk Navy Base in Virginia. This was the next stepping stone in the career of a military officer. Its purpose was to train officers to become general staff officers in Joint Commands, involving all of the military services. It was the point at which my life changed from a singular army career, into one which was more varied and with much broader horizons.

It was planned that after graduation from the Armed Forces Staff College, I would be transferred back to Washington and given a six month sabbatical leave. The purpose was so that I could complete my graduate studies in International Relations at the University of Maryland. It was expected that after completing my studies, I would be given a "plush" assignment with the NATO Armed Forces in Europe.

However, once again, fate, or my guardian angel, intervened. I was not given a sabbatical leave nor a "plush" assignment with NATO. Instead, I and my family were dispatched immediately to Iran.

Hence, my entire life was changed.

So ends VOLUME I.

ACKNOWLEDGMENTS

This book could not have been written and published without the support and assistance of the following:

Rita Pfeifer; my sister, advisor, family historian, and memory bank.

Gordon & Bonnie Verro, Wizard of Ink Printing; for their technical advice, assistance, and most important, their patience.

Judy Jenkins and Almut Metzroth; proof readers.

John Maylie, Chief Cartographer

GOOGLE; that unequaled and invaluable electronic search engine.

US Army Signal Corps Museum, Robert Anzuoni, director.

Fort MacArthur Museum, Stephen Nelson, Director.

Office of Air Force History, Washington, D.C.

Naval Historical Center, Michael Crawford, Director.

US Army Air Defense Artillery Center, John Hamilton, Command Historian.

Art.com Inc., Print, Poster, and Custom Framing Center.

US Air Force Aeronautical Chart and Information Center, St. Louis, MO.

North American Aerospace Defense Command, Patricia M. Goude, Writer-Editor.

US Department of Defense Archives, Washington, D.C.

US Army Resources Command, Alexandria, VA.

US Army Aviation & Missile Command, Redstone Arsenal, Michael E. Baker, Command Historian.